With scent of flowers, the murmur of that folk
Wherethrough from time to time a song outbroke,
Till scarce they thought about the story due;
Yet, when anigh to sun-setting it grew,
A book upon the board an elder laid,
And turning from the open window said,
"Too fair a tale the lovely time doth ask,
For this of mine to be an easy task,
Yet in what words soever this is writ,
As for the matter, I dare say of it
That it is lovely as the lovely May;
Pass then the manner, since the learned say
No written record was there of the tale,
Ere we from our fair land of Greece set sail;
How this may be I know not, this I know
That such-like tales the wind would seem to blow
From place to place, e'en as the feathery seed
Is borne across the sea to help the need
Of barren isles; so, sirs, from seed thus sown,
This flower, a gift from other lands has grown.

THE STORY OF CUPID AND PSYCHE

ARGUMENT

Psyche, a king's daughter, by her exceeding beauty caused the people to forget Venus; therefore the goddess would fain have destroyed her: nevertheless she became the bride of Love, yet in an unhappy moment lost him by her own fault, and wandering through the world suffered many evils at the hands of Venus, for whom she must accomplish fearful tasks. But the gods and all nature helped her, and in process of time she was reunited to Love, forgiven by Venus, and made immortal by the   Father of gods and men.

In the Greek land of old there was a King
Happy in battle, rich in everything;
Most rich in this, that he a daughter had
Whose beauty made the longing city glad.
She was so fair, that strangers from the sea
Just landed, in the temples thought that she
Was Venus visible to mortal eyes,
New come from Cyprus for a world's surprise.
She was so beautiful that had she stood
On windy Ida by the oaken wood,
And bared her limbs to that bold shepherd's gaze,
Troy might have stood till now with happy days;
And those three fairest, all have left the land
And left her with the apple in her hand.

And Psyche is her name in stories old,
As ever by our fathers we were told.

All this beheld Queen Venus from her throne,
And felt that she no longer was alone
In beauty, but, if only for a while,
This maiden matched her god-enticing smile;
Therefore, she wrought in such a wise, that she,
If honoured as a goddess, certainly
Was dreaded as a goddess none the less,
And midst her wealth, dwelt long in loneliness.
Two sisters had she, and men deemed them fair,
But as King's daughters might be anywhere,
And these to men of name and great estate
Were wedded, while at home must Psyche wait.
The sons of kings before her silver feet
Still bowed, and sighed for her; in measures sweet
The minstrels to the people sung her praise,
Yet must she live a virgin all her days.

So to Apollo's fane her father sent,
Seeking to know the dreadful Gods' intent,
And therewith sent he goodly gifts of price
A silken veil, wrought with a paradise,
Three golden bowls, set round with many a gem,
Three silver robes, with gold in every hem,
And a fair ivory image of the god
That underfoot a golden serpent trod;
And when three lords with these were gone away,
Nor could return until the fortieth day,
Ill was the King at ease, and neither took
Joy in the chase, or in the pictured book
The skilled Athenian limner had just wrought,
Nor in the golden cloths from India brought.
At last the day came for those lords' return,
And then 'twixt hope and fear the King did burn,
As on his throne with great pomp he was set,
And by him Psyche, knowing not as yet
Why they had gone: thus waiting, at noontide
They in the palace heard a voice outside,
And soon the messengers came hurrying,
And with pale faces knelt before the King,
And rent their clothes, and each man on his head
Cast dust, the while a trembling courtier read
This scroll, wherein the fearful answer lay,
Whereat from every face joy passed away.

THE ORACLE
O father of a most unhappy maid,
O King, whom all the world henceforth shall know
As wretched among wretches, be afraid
To ask the gods thy misery to show,
But if thou needs must hear it, to thy woe

Take back thy gifts to feast thine eyes upon,
When thine own flesh and blood some beast hath won.

"For hear thy doom, a rugged rock there is
Set back a league from thine own palace fair,
There leave the maid, that she may wait the kiss
Of the fell monster that doth harbour there:
This is the mate for whom her yellow hair
And tender limbs have been so fashioned,
This is the pillow for her lovely head.

"O what an evil from thy loins shall spring,
For all the world this monster overturns,
He is the bane of every mortal thing,
And this world ruined, still for more he yearns;
A fire there goeth from his mouth that burns
Worse than the flame of Phlegethon the red
To such a monster shall thy maid be wed.

"And if thou sparest now to do this thing,
I will destroy thee and thy land also,
And of dead corpses shalt thou be the King,
And stumbling through the dark land shalt thou go,
Howling for second death to end thy woe;
Live therefore as thou mayst and do my will,
And be a King that men may envy still."

What man was there, whose face changed not for grief
At hearing this? Psyche, shrunk like the leaf
The autumn frost first touches on the tree,
Stared round about with eyes that could not see,
And muttered sounds from lips that said no word,
And still within her ears the sentence heard
When all was said and silence fell on all
'Twixt marble columns and adorned wall.
Then spoke the King, bowed down with misery:
"What help is left! O daughter, let us die,
Or else together fleeing from this land,
From town to town go wandering hand in hand
Thou and I, daughter, till all men forget
That ever on a throne I have been set,
And then, when houseless and disconsolate,
We ask an alms before some city gate,
The gods perchance a little gift may give,
And suffer thee and me like beasts to live."
Then answered Psyche, through her bitter tears,
"Alas! my father, I have known these years
That with some woe the gods have dowered me,
And weighed 'gainst riches infelicity;
Ill is it then against the gods to strive;
Live on, O father, those that are alive

May still be happy; would it profit me
To live awhile, and ere I died to see
Thee perish, and all folk who love me well,
And then at last be dragged myself to hell
Cursed of all men? nay, since all things must die,
And I have dreamed not of eternity,
Why weepest thou that I must die to-day?
Why weepest thou? cast thought of shame away.
The dead are not ashamed, they feel no pain;
I have heard folk who spoke of death as gain
And yet, ah, God, if I had been some maid,
Toiling all day, and in the night-time laid
Asleep on rushes, had I only died
Before this sweet life I had fully tried,
Upon that day when for my birth men sung,
And o'er the feasting folk the sweet bells rung."

And therewith she arose and gat away,
And in her chamber, mourning long she lay,
Thinking of all the days that might have been,
And how that she was born to be a queen,
The prize of some great conqueror of renown,
The joy of many a country and fair town,
The high desire of every prince and lord,
One who could fright with careless smile or word
The hearts of heroes fearless in the war,
The glory of the world, the leading-star
Unto all honour and all earthly fame
Round goes the wheel, and death and deadly shame
Shall be her lot, while yet of her men sing
Unwitting that the gods have done this thing.
Long time she lay there, while the sunbeams moved
Over her body through the flowers she loved;
And in the eaves the sparrows chirped outside,
Until for weariness she grew dry-eyed,
And into an unhappy sleep she fell.

But of the luckless King now must we tell,
Who sat devising means to 'scape that shame,
Until the frightened people thronging came
About the palace, and drove back the guards,
Making their way past all the gates and wards;
And, putting chamberlains and marshals by,
Surged round the very throne tumultuously.
Then knew the wretched King all folk had heard
The miserable sentence, and the word
The gods had spoken; and from out his seat
He rose, and spoke in humble words, unmeet
For a great King, and prayed them give him grace,
While 'twixt his words the tears ran down his face
On to his raiment stiff with golden thread.

But little heeded they the words he said,
For very fear had made them pitiless;
Nor cared they for the maid and her distress,
But clashed their spears together and 'gan cry:
"For one man's daughter shall the people die,
And this fair land become an empty name,
Because thou art afraid to meet the shame
Wherewith the gods reward thy hidden sin?
Nay, by their glory do us right herein!"
"Ye are in haste to have a poor maid slain,"
The King said; "but my will herein is vain,
For ye are many, I one aged man:
Let one man speak, if for his shame he can."
Then stepped a sturdy dyer forth, who said,
"Fear of the gods brings no shame, by my head.
Listen; thy daughter we would have thee leave
Upon the fated mountain this same eve;
And thither must she go right well arrayed
In marriage raiment, loose hair as a maid,
And saffron veil, and with her shall there go
Fair maidens bearing torches, two and two;
And minstrels, in such raiment as is meet
The god-ordainéd fearful spouse to greet.
So shalt thou save our wives and little ones,
And something better than a heap of stones,
Dwelt in by noisesome things, this town shall be,
And thou thyself shalt keep thy sovereignty;
But if thou wilt not do the thing I say,
Then shalt thou live in bonds from this same day,
And we will bear thy maid unto the hill,
And from the dread gods save the city still."
Then loud they shouted at the words he said,
And round the head of the unhappy maid,
Dreaming uneasily of long-past joys,
Floated the echo of that dreadful noise,
And changed her dreams to dreams of misery.
But when the King knew that the thing must be,
And that no help there was in this distress,
He bade them have all things in readiness
To take the maiden out at sun-setting,
And wed her to the unknown dreadful thing.
So through the palace passed with heavy cheer
Her women gathering the sad wedding gear,
Who lingering long, yet at the last must go,
To waken Psyche to her bitter woe.
So coming to her bower, they found her there,
From head to foot rolled in her yellow hair,
As in the saffron veil she should be soon
Betwixt the setting sun and rising moon;
But when above her a pale maiden bent
And touched her, from her heart a sigh she sent,

And waking, on their woeful faces stared,
Sitting upright, with one white shoulder bared
By writhing on the bed in wretchedness.
Then suddenly remembering her distress,
She bowed her head and 'gan to weep and wail
But let them wrap her in the bridal veil,
And bind the sandals to her silver feet,
And set the rose-wreath on her tresses sweet:
But spoke no word, yea, rather, wearily
Turned from the yearning face and pitying eye
Of any maid who seemed about to speak.
Now through the garden trees the sun 'gan break,
And that inevitable time drew near;
Then through the courts, grown cruel, strange, and drear,
Since the bright morn, they led her to the gate.
Where she beheld a golden litter wait.
Whereby the King stood, aged and bent to earth,
The flute-players with faces void of mirth,
The down-cast bearers of the ivory wands,
The maiden torch-bearers' unhappy bands.

So then was Psyche taken to the hill,
And through the town the streets were void and still;
For in their houses all the people stayed,
Of that most mournful music sore afraid.
But on the way a marvel did they see,
For, passing by, where wrought of ivory,
There stood the Goddess of the flowery isle,
All folk could see the carven image smile.
But when anigh the hill's bare top they came,
Where Psyche must be left to meet her shame,
They set the litter down, and drew aside
The golden curtains from the wretched bride,
Who at their bidding rose and with them went
Afoot amidst her maids with head down-bent,
Until they came unto the drear rock's brow;
And there she stood apart, not weeping now,
But pale as privet blossom is in June.
There as the quivering flutes left off their tune,
In trembling arms the weeping, haggard King
Caught Psyche, who, like some half-lifeless thing,
Took all his kisses, and no word could say,
Until at last perforce he turned away;
Because the longest agony has end,
And homeward through the twilight did they wend.

But Psyche, now faint and bewildered,
Remembered little of her pain and dread;
Her doom drawn nigh took all her fear away,
And left her faint and weary; as they say
It haps to one who 'neath a lion lies,

Who stunned and helpless feels not ere he dies
The horror of the yellow fell, the red
Hot mouth, and white teeth gleaming o'er his head;
So Psyche felt, as sinking on the ground
She cast one weary vacant look around,
And at the ending of that wretched day
Swooning beneath the risen moon she lay.

Now backward must our story go awhile
And unto Cyprus the fair flowered isle,
Where hid away from every worshipper
Was Venus sitting, and her son by her
Standing to mark what words she had to say,
While in his dreadful wings the wind did play:
Frowning she spoke, in plucking from her thigh
The fragrant flowers that clasped it lovingly.
"In such a town, O son, a maid there is
Whom any amorous man this day would kiss
As gladly as a goddess like to me,
And though I know an end to this must be,
When white and red and gold are waxen grey
Down on the earth, while unto me one day
Is as another; yet behold, my son,
And go through all my temples one by one
And look what incense rises unto me;
Hearken the talk of sailors from the sea
Just landed, ever will it be the same,
'Hast thou then seen her?' Yea, unto my shame
Within the temple that is calléd mine,
As through the veil I watched the altar shine
This happed; a man with outstretched hand there stood,
Glittering in arms, of smiling joyous mood,
With crisp, black hair, and such a face one sees
But seldom now, and limbs like Hercules;
But as he stood there in my holy place,
Across mine image came the maiden's face,
And when he saw her, straight the warrior said
Turning about unto an earthly maid,
'O, lady Venus, thou art kind to me
After so much of wandering on the sea
To show thy very body to me here,'
But when this impious saying I did hear,
I sent them a great portent, for straightway
I quenched the fire, and no priest on that day
Could light it any more for all his prayer.
"So must she fall, so must her golden hair
Flash no more through the city, or her feet
Be seen like lilies moving down the street;
No more must men watch her soft raiment cling
About her limbs, no more must minstrels sing
The praises of her arms and hidden breast.

And thou it is, my son, must give me rest
From all this worship wearisomely paid
Unto a mortal who should be afraid
To match the gods in beauty; take thy bow
And dreadful arrows, and about her sow
The seeds of folly, and with such an one
I pray thee cause her mingle, fair my son,
That not the poorest peasant girl in Greece
Would look on for the gift of Jason's fleece.
Do this, and see thy mother glad again,
And free from insult, in her temples reign
Over the hearts of lovers in the spring."

"Mother," he said, "thou askest no great thing,
Some wretch too bad for death I soon shall find,
Who round her perfect neck his arms shall wind.
She shall be driven from the palace gate
Where once her crowd of worshippers would wait
From earliest morning till the dew was dry
On chance of seeing her gold gown glancing by;
There through the storm of curses shall she go
In evil raiment midst the winter snow,
Or in the summer in rough sheepskins clad.
And thus, O mother, shall I make thee glad
Remembering all the honour thou hast brought
Unto mine altars; since as thine own thought
My thought is grown, my mind as thy dear mind."

Then straight he rose from earth and down the wind
Went glittering 'twixt the blue sky and the sea,
And so unto the place came presently
Where Psyche dwelt, and through the gardens fair
Passed seeking her, and as he wandered there
Had still no thought but to do all her will,
Nor cared to think if it were good or ill:
So beautiful and pitiless he went,
And toward him still the blossomed fruit-trees leant,
And after him the wind crept murmuring,
And on the boughs the birds forgot to sing.

Withal at last amidst a fair green close,
Hedged round about with woodbine and red rose,
Within the flicker of a white-thorn shade
In gentle sleep he found the maiden laid
One hand that held a book had fallen away
Across her body, and the other lay
Upon a marble fountain's plashing rim,
Among whose broken waves the fish showed dim,
But yet its wide-flung spray now woke her not,
Because the summer day at noon was hot,
And all sweet sounds and scents were lulling her.

So soon the rustle of his wings 'gan stir
Her looser folds of raiment, and the hair
Spread wide upon the grass and daisies fair,
As Love cast down his eyes with a half smile
Godlike and cruel; that faded in a while,
And long he stood above her hidden eyes
With red lips parted in a god's surprise.

Then very Love knelt down beside the maid
And on her breast a hand unfelt he laid,
And drew the gown from off her dainty feet,
And set his fair cheek to her shoulder sweet,
And kissed her lips that knew of no love yet,
And wondered if his heart would e'er forget
The perfect arm that o'er her body lay.

But now by chance a damsel came that way,
One of her ladies, and saw not the god,
Yet on his shafts cast down had well-nigh trod
In wakening Psyche, who rose up in haste
And girded up her gown about her waist,
And with that maid went drowsily away.

From place to place Love followed her that day
And ever fairer to his eyes she grew,
So that at last when from her bower he flew,
And underneath his feet the moonlit sea
Went shepherding his waves disorderly,
He swore that of all gods and men, no one
Should hold her in his arms but he alone;
That she should dwell with him in glorious wise
Like to a goddess in some paradise;
Yea, he would get from Father Jove this grace
That she should never die, but her sweet face
And wonderful fair body should endure
Till the foundations of the mountains sure
Were molten in the sea; so utterly
Did he forget his mother's cruelty.

And now that he might come to this fair end,
He found Apollo, and besought him lend
His throne of divination for a while,
Whereby he did the priestess there beguile,
To give the cruel answer ye have heard
Unto those lords, who wrote it word by word,
And back unto the King its threatenings bore,
Whereof there came that grief and mourning sore,
Of which ye wot; thereby is Psyche laid
Upon the mountain-top; thereby, afraid
Of some ill yet, within the city fair
Cower down the people that have sent her there.

Withal did Love call unto him the Wind
Called Zephyrus, who most was to his mind,
And said, "O rainy wooer of the spring,
I pray thee, do for me an easy thing;
To such a hill-top go, O gentle Wind,
And there a sleeping maiden shalt thou find;
Her perfect body in thine arms with care
Take up, and unto the green valley bear
That lies before my noble house of gold;
There leave her lying on the daisies cold."
Then, smiling, toward the place the fair Wind went
While 'neath his wing the sleeping lilies bent,
And flying 'twixt the green earth and the sea
Made the huge anchored ships dance merrily,
And swung round from the east the gilded vanes
On many a palace, and from unhorsed wains
Twitched off the wheat-straw in his hurried flight;
But ere much time had passed he came in sight
Of Psyche laid in swoon upon the hill,
And smiling, set himself to do Love's will;
For in his arms he took her up with care,
Wondering to see a mortal made so fair,
And came into the vale in little space,
And set her down in the most flowery place;
And then unto the plains of Thessaly
Went ruffling up the edges of the sea.

Now underneath the world the moon was gone,
But brighter shone the stars so left alone,
Until a faint green light began to show
Far in the east, whereby did all men know,
Who lay awake either with joy or pain,
That day was coming on their heads again;
Then widening, soon it spread to grey twilight,
And in a while with gold the east was bright;
The birds burst out a-singing one by one,
And o'er the hill-top rose the mighty sun.
Therewith did Psyche open wide her eyes,
And rising on her arm, with great surprise
Gazed on the flowers wherein so deep she lay,
And wondered why upon that dawn of day
Out in the fields she had lift up her head
Rather than in her balmy gold-hung bed.
Then, suddenly remembering all her woes,
She sprang upon her feet, and yet arose
Within her heart a mingled hope and dread
Of some new thing: and now she raised her head,
And gazing round about her timidly,
A lovely grassy valley could she see,
That steep grey cliffs upon three sides did bound,

And under these, a river sweeping round,
With gleaming curves the valley did embrace,
And seemed to make an island of that place;
And all about were dotted leafy trees,
The elm for shade, the linden for the bees,
The noble oak, long ready for the steel
Which in that place it had no fear to feel;
The pomegranate, the apple, and the pear,
That fruit and flowers at once made shift to bear,
Nor yet decayed therefor, and in them hung
Bright birds that elsewhere sing not, but here sung
As sweetly as the small brown nightingales
Within the wooded, deep Laconian vales.
But right across the vale, from side to side,
A high white wall all further view did hide,
But that above it, vane and pinnacle
Rose up, of some great house beyond to tell,
And still betwixt these, mountains far away
Against the sky rose shadowy, cold, and grey.

She, standing in the yellow morning sun,
Could scarcely think her happy life was done,
Or that the place was made for misery;
Yea, some lone heaven it rather seemed to be,
Which for the coming band of gods did wait;
Hope touched her heart; no longer desolate,
Deserted of all creatures did she feel,
And o'er her face sweet colour 'gan to steal,
That deepened to a flush, as wandering thought
Desires before unknown unto her brought,
So mighty was the God, though far away.
But trembling midst her hope, she took her way
Unto a little door midmost the wall,
And still on odorous flowers her feet did fall,
And round about her did the strange birds sing,
Praising her beauty in their carolling.
Thus coming to the door, when now her hand
First touched the lock, in doubt she needs must stand,
And to herself she said, "Lo, here the trap!
And yet, alas! whatever now may hap,
How can I 'scape the ill which waiteth me?
Let me die now!" and herewith, tremblingly,
She raised the latch, and her sweet sinless eyes
Beheld a garden like a paradise,
Void of mankind, fairer than words can say,
Wherein did joyous harmless creatures play
After their kind, and all amidst the trees
Were strange-wrought founts and wondrous images;
And glimmering 'twixt the boughs could she behold
A house made beautiful with beaten gold,
Whose open doors in the bright sun did gleam;

Lonely, but not deserted did it seem.
Long time she stood debating what to do,
But at the last she passed the wicket through,
Which, shutting clamorously behind her, sent
A pang of fear throughout her as she went;
But when through all that green place she had passed
And by the palace porch she stood at last,
And saw how wonderfully the wall was wrought,
With curious stones from far-off countries brought,
And many an image and fair history
Of what the world has been, and yet shall be,
And all set round with golden craftsmanship,
Well-wrought as some renowned cup's royal lip,
She had a thought again to turn aside:
And yet again, not knowing where to bide,
She entered softly, and with trembling hands
Holding her gown; the wonder of all lands
Met there the wonders of the land and sea.

Now went she through the chambers tremblingly,
And oft in going would she pause and stand,
And drop the gathered raiment from her hand,
Stilling the beating of her heart for fear
As voices whispering low she seemed to hear,
But then again the wind it seemed to be
Moving the golden hangings doubtfully,
Or some bewildered swallow passing close
Unto the pane, or some wind-beaten rose.
Soon seeing that no evil thing came near,
A little she began to lose her fear,
And gaze upon the wonders of the place,
And in the silver mirrors saw her face
Grown strange to her amidst that loneliness,
And stooped to feel the web her feet did press,
Wrought by the brown slim-fingered Indian's toil
Amidst the years of war and vain turmoil;
Or she the figures of the hangings felt,
Or daintily the unknown blossoms smelt,
Or stood and pondered what new thing might mean
The images of knight and king and queen
Wherewith the walls were pictured here and there,
Or touched rich vessels with her fingers fair,
And o'er her delicate smooth cheek would pass
The long-fixed bubbles of strange works of glass:
So wandered she amidst these marvels new
Until anigh the noontide now it grew.
At last she came unto a chamber cool
Paved cunningly in manner of a pool,
Where red fish seemed to swim through floating weed
And at the first she thought it so indeed,
And took the sandals quickly from her feet,

But when the glassy floor these did but meet
The shadow of a long-forgotten smile
Her anxious face a moment did beguile;
And crossing o'er, she found a table spread
With dainty food, as delicate white bread
And fruits piled up and covered savoury meat,
As though a king were coming there to eat,
For the worst vessel was of beaten gold.
Now when these dainties Psyche did behold
She fain had eaten, but did nowise dare,
Thinking she saw a god's feast lying there.
But as she turned to go the way she came
She heard a low soft voice call out her name,
Then she stood still, and trembling gazed around,
And seeing no man, nigh sank upon the ground,
Then through the empty air she heard the voice.

"O, lovely one, fear not! rather rejoice
That thou art come unto thy sovereignty:
Sit now and eat, this feast is but for thee,
Yea, do whatso thou wilt with all things here,
And in thine own house cast away thy fear,
For all is thine, and little things are these
So loved a heart as thine, awhile to please.
"Be patient! thou art loved by such an one
As will not leave thee mourning here alone,
But rather cometh on this very night;
And though he needs must hide him from thy sight
Yet all his words of love thou well mayst hear,
And pour thy woes into no careless ear.
"Bethink thee then, with what solemnity
Thy folk, thy father, did deliver thee
To him who loves thee thus, and void of dread
Remember, sweet, thou art a bride new-wed."

Now hearing this, did Psyche, trembling sore
And yet with lighter heart than heretofore,
Sit down and eat, till she grew scarce afeard;
And nothing but the summer noise she heard
Within the garden, then, her meal being done,
Within the window-seat she watched the sun
Changing the garden-shadows, till she grew
Fearless and happy, since she deemed she knew
The worst that could befall, while still the best
Shone a fair star far off: and mid the rest
This brought her after all her grief and fear,
She said, "How sweet it would be, could I hear,
Soft music mate the drowsy afternoon,
And drown awhile the bees' sad murmuring tune
Within these flowering limes." E'en as she spoke,
A sweet-voiced choir of unknown unseen folk

Singing to words that match the sense of these
Hushed the faint music of the linden trees.

SONG

O pensive, tender maid, downcast and shy,
Who turnest pale e'en at the name of love,
And with flushed face must pass the elm-tree by
Ashamed to hear the passionate grey dove
Moan to his mate, thee too the god shall move,
Thee too the maidens shall ungird one day,
And with thy girdle put thy shame away.

What then, and shall white winter ne'er be done
Because the glittering frosty morn is fair?
Because against the early-setting sun
Bright show the gilded boughs though waste and bare?
Because the robin singeth free from care?
Ah! these are memories of a better day
When on earth's face the lips of summer lay.

Come then, beloved one, for such as thee
Love loveth, and their hearts he knoweth well,
Who hoard their moments of felicity,
As misers hoard the medals that they tell,
Lest on the earth but paupers they should dwell:
"We hide our love to bless another day;
The world is hard, youth passes quick," they say.

Ah, little ones, but if ye could forget
Amidst your outpoured love that you must die,
Then ye, my servants, were death's conquerors yet,
And love to you should be eternity
How quick soever might the days go by:
Yes, ye are made immortal on the day
Ye cease the dusty grains of time to weigh.

Thou hearkenest, love? O, make no semblance then
That thou art loved, but as thy custom is
Turn thy grey eyes away from eyes of men,
With hands down-dropped, that tremble with thy bliss,
With hidden eyes, take thy first lover's kiss;
Call this eternity which is to-day,
Nor dream that this our love can pass away.

They ceased, and Psyche pondering o'er their song,
Not fearing now that aught would do her wrong,
About the chambers wandered at her will,
And on the many marvels gazed her fill,
Where'er she passed still noting everything,
Then in the gardens heard the new birds sing

And watched the red fish in the fountains play,
And at the very faintest time of day
Upon the grass lay sleeping for a while
Midst heaven-sent dreams of bliss that made her smile;
And when she woke the shades were lengthening,
So to the place where she had heard them sing
She came again, and through a little door
Entered a chamber with a marble floor,
Open a-top unto the outer air,
Beneath which lay a bath of water fair,
Paved with strange stones and figures of bright gold,
And from the steps thereof could she behold
The slim-leaved trees against the evening sky
Golden and calm, still moving languidly.
So for a time upon the brink she sat,
Debating in her mind of this and that,
And then arose and slowly from her cast
Her raiment, and adown the steps she passed
Into the water, and therein she played,
Till of herself at last she grew afraid,
And of the broken image of her face,
And the loud splashing in that lonely place.
So from the bath she gat her quietly,
And clad herself in whatso haste might be;
And when at last she was apparelled
Unto a chamber came, where was a bed
Of gold and ivory, and precious wood
Some island bears where never man has stood;
And round about hung curtains of delight,
Wherein were interwoven Day and Night
Joined by the hands of Love, and round their wings
Knots of fair flowers no earthly May-time brings.
Strange for its beauty was the coverlet,
With birds and beasts and flowers wrought over it;
And every cloth was made in daintier wise
Than any man on earth could well devise:
Yea, there such beauty was in everything,
That she, the daughter of a mighty king,
Felt strange therein, and trembled lest that she,
Deceived by dreams, had wandered heedlessly
Into a bower for some fair goddess made.
Yet if perchance some man had thither strayed,
It had been long ere he had noted aught
But her sweet face, made pensive by the thought
Of all the wonders that she moved in there.
But looking round, upon a table fair
She saw a book wherein old tales were writ,
And by the window sat, to read in it
Until the dusk had melted into night,
When waxen tapers did her servants light
With unseen hands, until it grew like day.

And so at last upon the bed she lay,
And slept a dreamless sleep for weariness,
Forgetting all the wonder and distress.

But at the dead of night she woke, and heard
A rustling noise, and grew right sore afeard,
Yea, could not move a finger for affright;
And all was darker now than darkest night.

Withal a voice close by her did she hear.
"Alas, my love! why tremblest thou with fear,
While I am trembling with new happiness?
Forgive me, sweet, thy terror and distress:
Not otherwise could this our meeting be.
O loveliest! such bliss awaiteth thee,
For all thy trouble and thy shameful tears.
Such nameless honour, and such happy years,
As fall not unto women of the earth.
Loved as thou art, thy short-lived pains are worth
The glory and the joy unspeakable
Wherein the Treasure of the World shall dwell:
A little hope, a little patience yet,
Ere everything thou wilt, thou may'st forget,
Or else remember as a well-told tale,
That for some pensive pleasure may avail.
Canst thou not love me, then, who wrought thy woe,
That thou the height and depth of joy mightst know?"

He spoke, and as upon the bed she lay,
Trembling amidst new thoughts, he sent a ray
Of finest love unto her inmost heart,
Till, murmuring low, she strove the night to part,
And like a bride who meets her love at last,
When the long days of yearning are o'erpast,
She reached to him her perfect arms unseen,
And said, "O Love, how wretched I have been!
What hast thou done?" And by her side he lay.
Till just before the dawning of the day.

The sun was high when Psyche woke again,
And turning to the place where he had lain
And seeing no one, doubted of the thing
That she had dreamed it, till a fair gold ring,
Unseen before, upon her hand she found,
And touching her bright head she felt it crowned
With a bright circlet; then withal she sighed.
And wondered how the oracle had lied,
And wished her father knew it, and straightway
Rose up and clad herself. Slow went the day,
Though helped with many a solace, till came night;
And therewithal the new, unseen delight,

She learned to call her Love.

So passed away
The days and nights, until upon a day
As in the shade, at noon she lay asleep.
She dreamed that she beheld her sisters weep,
And her old father clad in sorry guise,
Grown foolish with the weight of miseries,
Her friends black-clad and moving mournfully,
And folk in wonder landed from the sea,
At such a fall of such a matchless maid,
And in some press apart her raiment laid
Like precious relics, and an empty tomb
Set in the palace telling of her doom.
Therefore she wept in sleep, and woke with tears
Still on her face, and wet hair round her ears,
And went about unhappily that day,
Framing a gentle speech wherewith to pray
For leave to see her sisters once again,
That they might know her happy, and her pain
Turned all to joy, and honour come from shame.
And so at last night and her lover came,
And midst their fondling, suddenly she said,
"O Love, a little time we have been wed,
And yet I ask a boon of thee this night."
"Psyche," he said, "if my heart tells me right,
This thy desire may bring us bitter woe,
For who the shifting chance of fate can know?
Yet, forasmuch as mortal hearts are weak,
To-morrow shall my folk thy sisters seek,
And bear them hither; but before the day
Is fully ended must they go away.
And thou, beware, for, fresh and good and true,
Thou knowest not what worldly hearts may do,
Or what a curse gold is unto the earth.
Beware lest from thy full heart, in thy mirth,
Thou tell'st the story of thy love unseen:
Thy loving, simple heart, fits not a queen."
Then by her kisses did she know he frowned,
But close about him her fair arms she wound,
Until for happiness he 'gan to smile,
And in those arms forgat all else awhile.

So the next day, for joy that they should come,
Would Psyche further deck her strange new home,
And even as she 'gan to think the thought,
Quickly her will by unseen hands was wrought,
Who came and went like thoughts. Yea, how should I
Tell of the works of gold and ivory,
The gems and images, those hands brought there
The prisoned things of earth, and sea, and air,

They brought to please their mistress? Many a beast,
Such as King Bacchus in his reckless feast
Makes merry with, huge elephants, snow-white
With gilded tusks, or dusky-grey with bright
And shining chains about their wrinkled necks;
The mailed rhinoceros, that of nothing recks;
Dusky-maned lions; spotted leopards fair
That through the cane-brake move, unseen as air;
The deep-mouthed tiger, dread of the brown man;
The eagle, and the peacock, and the swan
These be the nobles of the birds and beasts.
But therewithal, for laughter at their feasts,
They brought them the gods' jesters, such as be
Quick-chattering apes, that yet in mockery
Of anxious men wrinkle their ugly brows;
Strange birds with pouches, birds with beaks like prows
Of merchant-ships, with tufted crests like threads,
With unimaginable monstrous heads.
Lo, such as these, in many a gilded cage
They brought, or chained for fear of sudden rage.
Then strewed they scented branches on the floor,
And hung rose-garlands up by the great door,
And wafted incense through the bowers and halls,
And hung up fairer hangings on the walls,
And filled the baths with water fresh and clear,
And in the chambers laid apparel fair,
And spread a table for a royal feast.
Then when from all these labours they had ceased,
Psyche they sung to sleep with lullabies;
Who slept not long, but opening soon her eyes,
Beheld her sisters on the threshold stand:
Then did she run to take them by the hand,
And laid her cheek to theirs, and murmured words
Of little meaning, like the moan of birds,
While they bewildered stood and gazed around,
Like people who in some strange land have found
One that they thought not of; but she at last
Stood back, and from her face the strayed locks cast,
And, smiling through her tears, said, "Ah, that ye
Should have to weep such useless tears for me!
Alas, the burden that the city bears
For nought! O me, my father's burning tears,
That into all this honour I am come!
Nay, does he live yet? Is the ancient home
Still standing? do the galleys throng the quays?
Do the brown Indians glitter down the ways
With rubies as of old? Yes, yes, ye smile,
For ye are thinking, but a little while
Apart from these has she been dwelling here;
Truly, yet long enough, loved ones and dear,
To make me other than I was of old,

Though now when your dear faces I behold
Am I myself again. But by what road
Have ye been brought to this my new abode?"
"Sister," said one, "I rose up from my bed
It seems this morn, and being apparelléd,
And walking in my garden, in a swoon
Helpless and unattended I sank down,
Wherefrom I scarce am waked, for as a dream
Dost thou with all this royal glory seem,
But for thy kisses and thy words, O love."
"Yea, Psyche," said the other, "as I drove
The ivory shuttle through the shuttle-race,
All was changed suddenly, and in this place
I found myself, and standing on my feet,
Where me with sleepy words this one did greet.
Now, sister, tell us whence these wonders come
With all the godlike splendour of your home."

"Sisters," she said, "more marvels shall ye see
When ye, have been a little while with me,
Whereof I cannot tell you more than this
That 'midst them all I dwell in ease and bliss,
Well loved and wedded to a mighty lord,
Fair beyond measure, from whose loving word
I know that happier days await me yet.
But come, my sisters, let us now forget
To seek for empty knowledge; ye shall take
Some little gifts for your lost sister's sake;
And whatso wonders ye may see or hear
Of nothing frightful have ye any fear."
Wondering they went with her, and looking round,
Each in the other's eyes a strange look found,
For these, her mother's daughters, had no part
In her divine fresh singleness of heart,
But longing to be great, remembered not
How short a time one heart on earth has got.
But keener still that guarded look now grew
As more of that strange lovely place they knew,
And as with growing hate, but still afeard,
The unseen choirs' heart-softening strains they heard,
Which did but harden these; and when at noon
They sought the shaded waters' freshening boon,
And all unhidden once again they saw
That peerless beauty, free from any flaw,
Which now at last had won its precious meed,
Her kindness then but fed the fire of greed
Within their hearts, her gifts, the rich attire
Wherewith she clad them, where like sparks of fire
The many-coloured gems shone midst the pearls
The soft silks' winding lines, the work of girls
By the Five Rivers; their fair marvellous crowns,

Their sandals' fastenings worth the rent of towns,
Zones and carved rings, and nameless wonders fair,
All things her faithful slaves had brought them there,
Given amid kisses, made them not more glad;
Since in their hearts the ravening worm they had
That love slays not, nor yet is satisfied
While aught but he has aught; yet still they tried
To look as they deemed loving folk should look,
And still with words of love her bounty took.

So at the last all being apparelléd,
Her sisters to the banquet Psyche led,
Fair were they, and each seemed a glorious queen
With all that wondrous daintiness beseen,
But Psyche clad in gown of dusky blue
Little adorned, with deep grey eyes that knew
The hidden marvels of Love's holy fire,
Seemed like the soul of innocent desire,
Shut from the mocking world, wherefrom those twain
Seemed come to lure her thence with labour vain.

Now having reached the place where they should eat,
Ere 'neath the canopy the three took seat,
The eldest sister unto Psyche said,
"And he, dear love, the man that thou hast wed,
Will he not wish to-day thy kin to see?
Then could we tell of thy felicity
The better, to our folk and father dear."
Then Psyche reddened, "Nay, he is not here,"
She stammered, "neither will be here to-day,
For mighty matters keep him far away."
"Alas!" the younger sister said, "Say then,
What is the likeness of this first of men;
What sayest thou about his loving eyne,
Are his locks black, or golden-red as thine?"
"Black-haired like me," said Psyche stammering,
And looking round, "what say I? like the king
Who rules the world, he seems to me at least
Come, sisters, sit, and let us make good feast!
My darling and my love ye shall behold
I doubt not soon, his crispy hair of gold,
His eyes unseen; and ye shall hear his voice,
That in my joy ye also may rejoice."

Then did they hold their peace, although indeed
Her stammering haste they did not fail to heed.
But at their wondrous royal feast they sat
Thinking their thoughts, and spoke of this or that
Between the bursts of music, until when
The sun was leaving the abodes of men;
And then must Psyche to her sisters say

That she was bid, her husband being away,
To suffer none at night to harbour there,
No, not the mother that her body bare
Or father that begat her, therefore they
Must leave her now, till some still happier day.
And therewithal more precious gifts she brought
Whereof not e'en in dreams they could have thought
Things whereof noble stories might be told;
And said; "These matters that you here behold
Shall be the worst of gifts that you shall have;
Farewell, farewell! and may the high gods save
Your lives and fame; and tell our father dear
Of all the honour that I live in here,
And how that greater happiness shall come
When I shall reach a long-enduring home."
Then these, though burning through the night to stay,
Spake loving words, and went upon their way,
When weeping she had kissed them; but they wept
Such tears as traitors do, for as they stepped
Over the threshold, in each other's eyes
They looked, for each was eager to surprise
The envy that their hearts were filled withal,
That to their lips came welling up like gall.

"So," said the first, "this palace without folk,
These wonders done with none to strike a stroke.
This singing in the air, and no one seen,
These gifts too wonderful for any queen,
The trance wherein we both were wrapt away,
And set down by her golden house to-day
These are the deeds of gods, and not of men;
And fortunate the day was to her, when
Weeping she left the house where we were born,
And all men deemed her shamed and most forlorn."
Then said the other, reddening in her rage,
"She is the luckiest one of all this age;
And yet she might have told us of her case,
What god it is that dwelleth in the place,
Nor sent us forth like beggars from her gate.
And beggarly, O sister, is our fate,
Whose husbands wring from miserable hinds
What the first battle scatters to the winds;
While she to us whom from her door she drives
And makes of no account or honour, gives
Such wonderful and priceless gifts as these,
Fit to bedeck the limbs of goddesses!
And yet who knows but she may get a fall?
The strongest tower has not the highest wall,
Think well of this, when you sit safe at home
By this unto the river were they come,
Where waited Zephyrus unseen, who cast

A languor over them that quickly passed
Into deep sleep, and on the grass they sank;
Then straightway did he lift them from the bank,
And quickly each in her fair house set down,
Then flew aloft above the sleeping town.
Long in their homes they brooded over this,
And how that Psyche nigh a goddess is;
While all folk deemed that she quite lost had been
For nought they said of all that they had seen.

But now that night when she, with many a kiss,
Had told their coming, and of that and this
That happed, he said, "These things, O Love, are well;
Glad am I that no evil thing befell.
And yet, between thy father's house and me
Must thou choose now; then either royally
Shalt thou go home, and wed some king at last,
And have no harm for all that here has passed;
Or else, my love, bear as thy brave heart may,
This loneliness in hope of that fair day,
Which, by my head, shall come to thee; and then
Shalt thou be glorious to the sons of men,
And by my side shalt sit in such estate
That in all time all men shall sing thy fate."
But with that word such love through her he breathed,
That round about him her fair arms she wreathed;
And so with loving passed the night away,
And with fresh hope came on the fresh May-day.
And so passed many a day and many a night.
And weariness was balanced with delight,
And into such a mind was Psyche brought,
That little of her father's house she thought,
But ever of the happy day to come
When she should go unto her promised home.

Till she that threw the golden apple down
Upon the board, and lighted up Troy town,
On dusky wings came flying o'er the place,
And seeing Psyche with her happy face
Asleep beneath some fair tree blossoming,
Into her sleep straight cast an evil thing;
Whereby she dreamed she saw her father laid
Panting for breath beneath the golden shade
Of his great bed's embroidered canopy,
And with his last breath moaning heavily
Her name and fancied woes; thereat she woke,
And this ill dream through all her quiet broke,
And when next morn her Love from her would go,
And going, as it was his wont to do,
Would kiss her sleeping, he must find the tears
Filling the hollows of her rosy ears

And wetting half the golden hair that lay
Twixt him and her: then did he speak and say,
"O Love, why dost thou lie awake and weep,
Who for content shouldst have good heart to sleep
This cold hour ere the dawning?" Nought she said,
But wept aloud. Then cried he, "By my head!
Whate'er thou wishest I will do for thee;
Yea, if it make an end of thee and me."
"O Love," she said, "I scarce dare ask again,
Yet is there in mine heart an aching pain
To know what of my father is become:
So would I send my sisters to my home,
Because I doubt indeed they never told
Of all my honour in this house of gold;
And now of them a great oath would I take."
He said, "Alas! and hast thou been awake
For them indeed? who in my arms asleep
Mightst well have been; for their sakes didst thou weep,
Who mightst have smiled to feel my kiss on thee?
Yet as thou wishest once more shall it be,
Because my oath constrains me, and thy tears.
And yet again beware, and make these fears
Of none avail; nor waver any more,
I pray thee: for already to the shore
Of all delights and joys thou drawest nigh."

He spoke, and from the chamber straight did fly
To highest heaven, and going softly then,
Wearied the father of all gods and men
With prayers for Psyche's immortality.

Meantime went Zephyrus across the sea,
To bring her sisters to her arms again,
Though of that message little was he fain,
Knowing their malice and their cankered hearts.
For now these two had thought upon their parts
And made up a false tale for Psyche's ear;
For when awaked, to her they drew anear,
Sobbing, their faces in their hands they hid,
Nor when she asked them why this thing they did
Would answer aught, till trembling Psyche said,
"Nay, nay, what is it? is our father dead?
Or do ye weep these tears for shame that ye
Have told him not of my felicity,
To make me weep amidst my new-found bliss?
Be comforted, for short the highway is
To my forgiveness: this day shall ye go
And take him gifts, and tell him all ye know
Of this my unexpected happy lot."
Amidst fresh sobs one said, "We told him not
But by good counsel did we hide the thing,

Deeming it well that he should feel the sting
For once, than for awhile be glad again,
And after come to suffer double pain."
"Alas! what mean you, sister?" Psyche said,
For terror waxing pale as are the dead.
"O sister, speak!" "Child, by this loving kiss,"
Spake one of them, "and that remembered bliss
We dwelt in when our mother was alive,
Or ever we began with ills to strive,
By all the hope thou hast to see again
Our aged father and to soothe his pain,
I charge thee tell me, Hast thou seen the thing
Thou callest Husband?"
Breathless, quivering,
Psyche cried out, "Alas! what sayest thou?
What riddles wilt thou speak unto me now?"
"Alas!" she said; "then is it as I thought.
Sister, in dreadful places have we sought
To learn about thy case, and thus we found
A wise man, dwelling underneath the ground
In a dark awful cave: he told to us
A horrid tale thereof, and piteous,
That thou wert wedded to an evil thing,
A serpent-bodied fiend of poisonous sting,
Bestial of form, yet therewith lacking not
E'en such a soul as wicked men have got.
Thus ages long agone the gods made him,
And set him in a lake hereby to swim;
But every hundred years he hath this grace,
That he may change within this golden place
Into a fair young man by night alone.
Alas, my sister, thou hast cause to groan!
What sayest thou? His words are fair and soft;
He raineth loving kisses on me oft,
Weeping for love; he tells me of a day
When from this place we both shall go away,
And he shall kiss me then no more unseen,
The while I sit by him a glorious queen
Alas, poor child! it pleaseth thee, his kiss?
Then must I show thee why he doeth this:
Because he willeth for a time to save
Thy body, wretched one! that he may have
Both child and mother for his watery hell
Ah, what a tale this is for me to tell!
"Thou prayest us to save thee, and we can;
Since for nought else we sought that wise old man,
Who for great gifts and seeing that of kings
We both were come, has told us all these things,
And given us a fair lamp of hallowed oil
That he has wrought with danger and much toil;
And thereto has he added a sharp knife,

In forging which he well-nigh lost his life,
About him so the devils of the pit
Came swarming, O, my sister, hast thou it?"
Straight from her gown the other one drew out
The lamp and knife, which Psyche, dumb with doubt
And misery at once, took in her hand.
Then said her sister, "From this doubtful land
Thou gav'st us royal gifts a while ago,
But these we give thee, though they lack for show,
Shall be to thee a better gift, thy life.
Put now in some sure place this lamp and knife,
And when he sleeps rise silently from bed
And hold the hallowed lamp above his head,
And swiftly draw the charmèd knife across
His cursed neck, thou well may'st bear the loss,
Nor shall he keep his man's shape more, when he
First feels the iron wrought so mysticly:
But thou, flee unto us, we have a tale,
Of what has been thy lot within this vale,
When we have 'scaped therefrom, which we shall do
By virtue of strange spells the old man knew.
Farewell, sweet sister! here we may not stay,
Lest in returning he should pass this way;
But in the vale we will not fail to wait
Till thou art loosened from thine evil fate."
Thus went they, and for long they said not aught,
Fearful lest any should surprise their thought,
But in such wise had envy conquered fear,
That they were fain that eve to bide anear
Their sister's ruined home; but when they came
Unto the river, on them fell the same
Resistless languor they had felt before.
And from the blossoms of that flowery shore
Their sleeping bodies soon did Zephyr bear,
For other folk to hatch new ills and care.

But on the ground sat Psyche all alone,
The lamp and knife beside her, and no moan
She made, but silent let the long hours go,
Till dark night closed around her and her woe.
Then trembling she arose, for now drew near
The time of utter loneliness and fear,
And she must think of death, who until now
Had thought of ruined life, and love brought low;
And with, that thought, tormenting doubt there came,
And images of some unheard-of shame,
Until forlorn, entrapped of gods she felt,
As though in some strange hell her spirit dwelt.
Yet driven by her sisters' words at last,
And by remembrance of the time now past,
When she stood trembling, as the oracle

With all its fearful doom upon her fell,
She to her hapless wedding-chamber turned,
And while the waxen tapers freshly burned
She laid those dread gifts ready to her hand,
Then quenched the lights, and by the bed did stand,
Turning these matters in her troubled mind;
And sometimes hoped some glorious man to find
Beneath the lamp, fit bridegroom for a bride
Like her; ah, then! with what joy to his side
Would she creep back in the dark silent night;
But whiles she quaked at thought of what a sight
The lamp might show her; the hot rush of blood
The knife might shed upon her as she stood,
The dread of some pursuit, the hurrying out,
Through rooms where every sound would seem a shout
Into the windy night among the trees,
Where many a changing monstrous sight one sees,
When nought at all has happed to chill the blood.

But as among these evil thoughts she stood,
She heard him coming, and straight crept to bed.
And felt him touch her with a new-born dread,
And durst not answer to his words of love.
But when he slept, she rose that tale to prove.
And sliding down as softly as might be,
And moving through the chamber quietly,
She gat the lamp within her trembling hand,
And long, debating of these things, did stand
In that thick darkness, till she seemed to be
A dweller in some black eternity,
And what she once had called the world did seem
A hollow void, a colourless mad dream;
For she felt so alone, three times in vain
She moved her heavy hand, three times again
It fell adown; at last throughout the place
Its flame glared, lighting up her woeful face,
Whose eyes the silken carpet did but meet,
Grown strange and awful, and her own wan feet
As toward the bed she stole; but come thereto
Back with dosed eyes and quivering lips, she threw
Her lovely head, and strove to think of it,
While images of fearful things did flit
Before her eyes; thus, raising up the hand
That bore the lamp, one moment did she stand
As man's time tells it, and then suddenly
Opened her eyes, but scarce kept back a cry
At what she saw; for there before her lay
The very Love brighter than dawn of day;
And as he lay there smiling, her own name
His gentle lips in sleep began to frame,
And as to touch her face his hand did move;

O then, indeed, her faint heart swelled for love,
And she began to sob, and tears fell fast
Upon the bed. But as she turned at last
To quench the lamp, there happed a little thing
That quenched her new delight, for flickering
The treacherous flame cast on his shoulder fair
A burning drop; he woke, and seeing her there
The meaning of that sad sight knew full well,
Nor was there need the piteous tale to tell.

Then on her knees she fell with a great cry,
For in his face she saw the thunder nigh,
And she began to know what she had done,
And saw herself henceforth, unloved, alone,
Pass onward to the grave; and once again
She heard the voice she now must love in vain
"Ah, has it come to pass? and hast thou lost
A life of love, and must thou still be tossed
One moment in the sun 'twixt night and night?
And must I lose what would have been delight,
Untasted yet amidst immortal bliss,
To wed a soul made worthy of my kiss,
Set in a frame so wonderfully made?
"O wavering heart, farewell! be not afraid
That I with fire will burn thy body fair,
Or cast thy sweet limbs piecemeal through the air;
The fates shall work thy punishment alone,
And thine own memory of our kindness done.
"Alas! what wilt thou do? how shalt thou bear
The cruel world, the sickening still despair,
The mocking, curious faces bent on thee,
When thou hast known what love there is in me?
O happy only, if thou couldst forget,
And live unholpen, lonely, loveless yet,
But untormented through the little span
That on the earth ye call the life of man.
Alas! that thou, too fair a thing to die,
Shouldst so be born to double misery!
"Farewell! though I, a god, can never know
How thou canst lose thy pain, yet time will go
Over thine head, and thou mayst mingle yet
The bitter and the sweet, nor quite forget,
Nor quite remember, till these things shall seem
The wavering memory of a lovely dream."
Therewith he caught his shafts up and his bow,
And striding through the chambers did he go,
Light all around him; and she, wailing sore,
Still followed after; but he turned no more,
And when into the moonlit night he came
From out her sight he vanished like a flame,
And on the threshold till the dawn of day

Through all the changes of the night she lay.

At daybreak when she lifted up her eyes,
She looked around with heavy dull surprise,
And rose to enter the fair golden place;
But then remembering all her piteous case
She turned away, lamenting very sore,
And wandered down unto the river shore;
There, at the head of a green pool and deep,
She stood so long that she forgot to weep,
And the wild things about the water-side
From such a silent thing cared not to hide;
The dace pushed 'gainst the stream, the dragon-fly,
With its green-painted wing, went flickering by;
The water-hen, the lustred kingfisher,
Went on their ways and took no heed of her;
The little reed birds never ceased to sing,
And still the eddy, like a living thing,
Broke into sudden gurgles at her feet.
But 'midst these fair things, on that morning sweet,
How could she, weary creature, find a place?
She moved at last, and lifting up her face,
Gathered her raiment up and cried, "Farewell,
O fairest lord! and since I cannot dwell
With thee in heaven, let me now hide my head
In whatsoever dark place dwell the dead!"
And with that word she leapt into the stream,
But the kind river even yet did deem
That she should live, and, with all gentle care,
Cast her ashore within a meadow fair.
Upon the other side, where Shepherd Pan
Sat looking down upon the water wan,
Goat-legged and merry, who called out, "Fair maid
Why goest thou hurrying to the feeble shade
Whence none return? Well do I know thy pain,
For I am old, and have not lived in vain;
Thou wilt forget all that within a while,
And on some other happy youth wilt smile;
And sure he must be dull indeed if he
Forget not all things in his ecstasy
At sight of such a wonder made for him,
That in that clinging gown makes mine eyes swim,
Old as I am: but to the god of Love
Pray now, sweet child, for all things can he move."
Weeping she passed him, but full reverently,
And well she saw that she was not to die
Till she had filled the measure of her woe.
So through the meads she passed, half blind and slow,
And on her sisters somewhat now she thought;
And, pondering on the evil they had wrought,
The veil fell from her, and she saw their guile.

"Alas!" she said, "can death make folk so vile?
What wonder that the gods are glorious then,
Who cannot feel the hates and fears of men?
Sisters, alas, for what ye used to be!
Once did I think, whatso might hap to me,
Still at the worst, within your arms to find
A haven of pure love; then were ye kind,
Then was your joy e'en as my very own
And now, and now, if I can be alone
That is my best: but that can never be,
For your unkindness still shall stay with me
When ye are dead. But thou, my love! my dear!
Wert thou not kind? I should have lost my fear
Within a little. Yea, and e'en just now
With angry godhead on thy lovely brow,
Still thou wert kind. And art thou gone away
For ever? I know not, but day by day
Still will I seek thee till I come to die,
And nurse remembrance of felicity
Within my heart, although it wound me sore;
For what am I but thine for evermore!"

Thenceforth her back upon the world she turned
As she had known it; in her heart there burned
Such deathless love, that still untired she went:
The huntsman dropping down the woody bent,
In the still evening, saw her passing by,
And for her beauty fain would draw anigh,
But yet durst not; the shepherd on the down
Wondering, would shade his eyes with fingers brown,
As on the hill's brow, looking o'er the lands,
She stood with straining eyes and clinging hands,
While the wind blew the raiment from her feet;
The wandering soldier her grey eyes would meet,
That took no heed of him, and drop his own;
Like a thin dream she passed the clattering town;
On the thronged quays she watched the ships come in
Patient, amid the strange outlandish din;
Unscared she saw the sacked towns' miseries,
And marching armies passed before her eyes.
And still of her the god had such a care
That none might wrong her, though alone and fair.
Through rough and smooth she wandered many a day,
Till all her hope had well-nigh passed away.

Meanwhile the sisters, each in her own home,
Waited the day when outcast she should come
And ask their pity; when perchance, indeed,
They looked to give her shelter in her need,
And with soft words such faint reproaches take
As she durst make them for her ruin's sake;

But day passed day, and still no Psyche came,
And while they wondered whether, to their shame,
Their plot had failed, or gained its end too well,
And Psyche slain, no tale thereof could tell.
Amidst these things, the eldest sister lay
Asleep one evening of a summer day,
Dreaming she saw the god of Love anigh,
Who seemed to say unto her lovingly,
"Hail unto thee, fair sister of my love;
Nor fear me for that thou her faith didst prove,
And found it wanting, for thou, too, art fair,
Nor is her place filled; rise, and have no care
For father or for friends, but go straightway
Unto the rock where she was borne that day;
There, if thou hast a will to be my bride,
Put thou all fear of horrid death aside,
And leap from off the cliff, and there will come
My slaves, to bear thee up and take thee home.
Haste then, before the summer night grows late,
For in my house thy beauty I await!"

So spake the dream; and through the night did sail,
And to the other sister bore the tale,
While this one rose, nor doubted of the thing,
Such deadly pride unto her heart did cling;
But by the tapers' light triumphantly,
Smiling, her mirrored body did she eye,
Then hastily rich raiment on her cast
And through the sleeping serving-people passed,
And looked with changed eyes on the moonlit street,
Nor scarce could feel the ground beneath her feet.
But long the time seemed to her, till she came
There where her sister once was borne to shame;
And when she reached the bare cliff's rugged brow
She cried aloud, "O Love, receive me now,
Who am not all unworthy to be thine!"
And with that word, her jewelled arms did shine
Outstretched beneath the moon, and with one breath
She sprung to meet the outstretched arms of Death,
The only god that waited for her there,
And in a gathered moment of despair
A hideous thing her traitrous life did seem.

But with the passing of that hollow dream
The other sister rose, and as she might,
Arrayed herself alone in that still night,
And so stole forth, and making no delay
Came to the rock anigh the dawn of day;
No warning there her sister's spirit gave,
No doubt came nigh the fore-doomed soul to save,
But with a fever burning in her blood,

With glittering eyes and crimson cheeks she stood
One moment on the brow, the while she cried,
"Receive me, Love, chosen to be thy bride
From all the million women of the world!"
Then o'er the cliff her wicked limbs were hurled,
Nor has the language of the earth a name
For that surprise of terror and of shame.

Now, midst her wanderings, on a hot noontide,
Psyche passed down a road, where, on each side
The yellow cornfields lay, although as yet
Unto the stalks no sickle had been set;
The lark sung over them, the butterfly
Flickered from ear to ear distractedly,
The kestrel hung above, the weasel peered
From out the wheat-stalks on her unafeard,
Along the road the trembling poppies shed
On the burnt grass their crumpled leaves and red;
Most lonely was it, nothing Psyche knew
Unto what land of all the world she drew;
Aweary was she, faint and sick at heart,
Bowed to the earth by thoughts of that sad part
She needs must play: some blue flower from the corn
That in her fingers erewhile she had borne,
Now dropped from them, still clung unto her gown;
Over the hard way hung her head adown
Despairingly, but still her weary feet
Moved on half conscious, her lost love to meet.
So going, at the last she raised her eyes,
And saw a grassy mound before her rise
Over the yellow plain, and thereon was
A marble fane with doors of burnished brass,
That 'twixt the pillars set about it burned;
So thitherward from off the road she turned,
And soon she heard a rippling water sound,
And reached a stream that girt the hill around,
Whose green waves wooed her body lovingly;
So looking round, and seeing no soul anigh,
Unclad, she crossed the shallows, and there laid
Her dusty raiment in the alder-shade,
And slipped adown into the shaded pool,
And with the pleasure of the water cool
Soothed her tired limbs awhile, then with a sigh
Came forth, and clad her body hastily,
And up the hill made for the little fane.
But when its threshold now her feet did gain,
She, looking through the pillars of the shrine,
Beheld therein a golden image shine
Of golden Ceres; then she passed the door,
And with bowed head she stood awhile before
The smiling image, striving for some word

That did not name her lover and her lord,
Until midst rising tears at last she prayed:
"O kind one, if while yet I was a maid
I ever did thee pleasure, on this day
Be kind to me, poor wanderer on the way,
Who strive my love upon the earth to meet!
Then let me rest my weary, doubtful feet
Within thy quiet house a little while,
And on my rest if thou wouldst please to smile,
And send me news of my own love and lord,
It would not cost thee, lady, many a word."
But straight from out the shrine a sweet voice came,
"O Psyche, though of me thou hast no blame,
And though indeed thou sparedst not to give
What my soul loved, while happy thou didst live,
Yet little can I give now unto thee,
Since thou art rebel, slave, and enemy
Unto the love-inspiring Queen; this grace
Thou hast alone of me, to leave this place
Free as thou camest, though the lovely one
Seeks for the sorceress who entrapped her son
In every land, and has small joy in aught,
Until before her presence thou art brought."
Then Psyche, trembling at the words she spake,
Durst answer nought, nor for that counsel's sake
Could other offerings leave except her tears,
As now, tormented by the new-born fears
The words divine had raised in her, she passed
The brazen threshold once again, and cast
A dreary hopeless look across the plain,
Whose golden beauty now seemed nought and vain
Unto her aching heart; then down the hill
She went, and crossed the shallows of the rill,
And wearily she went upon her way,
Nor any homestead passed upon that day,
Nor any hamlet, and at night lay down
Within a wood, far off from any town.

There, waking at the dawn, did she behold,
Through the green leaves, a glimmer as of gold,
And, passing on, amidst an oak-grove found
A pillared temple gold-adorned and round,
Whose walls were hung with rich and precious things,
Worthy to be the ransom of great kings;
And in the midst of gold and ivory
An image of Queen Juno did she see;
Then her heart swelled within her, and she thought,
"Surely the gods hereto my steps have brought,
And they will yet be merciful and give
Some little joy to me, that I may live
Till my Love finds me." Then upon her knees

She fell, and prayed, "O Crown of goddesses,
I pray thee, give me shelter in this place,
Nor turn away from me thy much-loved face,
If ever I gave golden gifts to thee
In happier times when my right hand was free."
Then from the inmost shrine there came a voice
That said, "It is so, well mayst thou rejoice
That of thy gifts I yet have memory,
Wherefore mayst thou depart forewarned and free;
Since she that won the golden apple lives,
And to her servants mighty gifts now gives
To find thee out, in whatso land thou art,
For thine undoing; loiter not, depart!
For what immortal yet shall shelter thee
From her that rose from out the unquiet sea?"
Then Psyche moaned out in her grief and fear,
"Alas! and is there shelter anywhere
Upon the green flame-hiding earth?" said she,
"Or yet beneath it is there peace for me?
O Love, since in thine arms I cannot rest,
Or lay my weary head upon thy breast,
Have pity yet upon thy love forlorn,
Make me as though I never had been born!"

Then wearily she went upon her way,
And so, about the middle of the day,
She came before a green and flowery place,
Walled round about in manner of a chase,
Whereof the gates as now were open wide;
Fair grassy glades and long she saw inside
Betwixt great trees, down which the unscared deer
Were playing; yet a pang of deadly fear,
She knew not why, shot coldly through her heart,
And thrice she turned as though she would depart,
And thrice returned, and in the gateway stood
With wavering feet: small flowers as red as blood
Were growing up amid the soft green grass,
And here and there a fallen rose there was,
And on the trodden grass a silken lace,
As though crowned revellers had passed by the place
The restless sparrows chirped upon the wall
And faint far music on her ears did fall,
And from the trees within, the pink-foot doves
Still told their weary tale unto their loves,
And all seemed peaceful more than words could say.
Then she, whose heart still whispered, "Keep away."
Was drawn by strong desire unto the place,
So toward the greenest glade she set her face,
Murmuring, "Alas! and what a wretch am I,
That I should fear the summer's greenery!
Yea, and is death now any more an ill,

When lonely through the world I wander still."
But when she was amidst those ancient groves,
Whose close green leaves and choirs of moaning doves
Shut out the world, then so alone she seemed,
So strange, her former life was but as dreamed;
Beside the hopes and fears that drew her on,
Till so far through that green place she had won,
That she a rose-hedged garden could behold
Before a house made beautiful with gold;
Which, to her mind beset with that past dream,
And dim foreshadowings of ill fate, did seem
That very house, her joy and misery,
Where that fair sight her longing eyes did see
They should not see again; but now the sound
Of pensive music echoing all around,
Made all things like a picture, and from thence
Bewildering odours floating, dulled her sense,
And killed her fear, and, urged by strong desire
To see how all should end, she drew yet nigher,
And o'er the hedge beheld the heads of girls
Embraced by garlands fresh and orient pearls,
And heard sweet voices murmuring; then a thrill
Of utmost joy all memory seemed to kill
Of good or evil, and her eager hand
Was on the wicket, then her feet did stand
Upon new flowers, the while her dizzied eyes
Gazed wildly round on half-seen mysteries,
And wandered from unnoting face to face.
For round a fountain midst the flowery place
Did she behold full many a minstrel girl;
While nigh them, on the grass in giddy whirl,
Bright raiment and white limbs and sandalled feet
Flew round in time unto the music sweet,
Whose strains no more were pensive now nor sad,
But rather a fresh sound of triumph had;
And round the dance were gathered damsels fair,
Clad in rich robes adorned with jewels rare;
Or little hidden by some woven mist,
That, hanging round them, here a bosom kissed
And there a knee, or driven by the wind
About some lily's bowing stem was twined.

But when a little Psyche's eyes grew clear,
A sight they saw that brought back all her fear
A hundred-fold, though neither heaven nor earth
To such a fair sight elsewhere could give birth;
Because apart, upon a golden throne
Of marvellous work, a woman sat alone,
Watching the dancers with a smiling face,
Whose beauty sole had lighted up the place.
A crown there was upon her glorious head,

A garland round about her girdlestead,
Where matchless wonders of the hidden sea
Were brought together and set wonderfully;
Naked she was of all else, but her hair
About her body rippled here and there,
And lay in heaps upon the golden seat,
And even touched the gold cloth where her feet
Lay amid roses, ah, how kind she seemed!
What depths of love from out her grey eyes beamed!

Well might the birds leave singing on the trees
To watch in peace that crown of goddesses,
Yet well might Psyche sicken at the sight,
And feel her feet wax heavy, her head light;
For now at last her evil day was come,
Since she had wandered to the very home
Of her most bitter cruel enemy.
Half-dead, yet must she turn about to flee,
But as her eyes back o'er her shoulder gazed,
And with weak hands her clinging gown she raised,
And from her lips unwitting came a moan,
She felt strong arms about her body thrown,
And, blind with fear, was haled along till she
Saw floating by her faint eyes dizzily
That vision of the pearls and roses fresh,
The golden carpet and the rosy flesh.
Then, as in vain she strove to make some sound,
A sweet voice seemed to pierce the air around
With bitter words; her doom rang in her ears,
She felt the misery that lacketh tears.
"Come hither, damsels, and the pearl behold
That hath no price? See now the thrice-tried gold,
That all men worshipped, that a god would have
To be his bride! how like a wretched slave
She cowers down, and lacketh even voice
To plead her cause! Come, damsels, and rejoice,
That now once more the waiting world will move,
Since she is found, the well-loved soul of love!
"And thou poor wretch, what god hath led thee here?
Art thou so lost in this abyss of fear,
Thou canst not weep thy misery and shame?
Canst thou not even speak thy shameful name?"

But even then the flame of fervent love
In Psyche's tortured heart began to move,
And gave her utterance, and she said, "Alas!
Surely the end of life has come to pass
For me, who have been bride of very Love,
Yet love still bides in me, O Seed of Jove,
For such I know thee; slay me, nought is lost!
For had I had the will to count the cost

And buy my love with all this misery,
Thus and no otherwise the thing should be.
Would I were dead, my wretched beauty gone,
No trouble now to thee or any one!"
And with that last word did she hang her head,
As one who hears not, whatsoe'er is said;
But Venus rising with a dreadful cry
Said, "O thou fool, I will not let thee die!
But thou shalt reap the harvest thou hast sown
And many a day thy wretched lot bemoan.
Thou art my slave, and not a day shall be
But I will find some fitting task for thee,
Nor will I slay thee till thou hop'st again.
What, thinkest thou that utterly in vain
Jove is my sire, and in despite my will
That thou canst mock me with thy beauty still?
Come forth, O strong-armed, punish this new slave,
That she henceforth a humble heart may have."
All round about the damsels in a ring
Were drawn to see the ending of the thing,
And now as Psyche's eyes stared wildly round
No help in any face of them she found
As from the fair and dreadful face she turned
In whose grey eyes such steadfast anger burned;
Yet midst her agony she scarcely knew
What thing it was the goddess bade them do,
And all the pageant, like a dreadful dream
Hopeless and long-enduring grew to seem;
Yea, when the strong-armed through the crowd did break,
Girls like to those, whose close-locked squadron shake
The echoing surface of the Asian plain,
And when she saw their threatening hands, in vain
She strove to speak, so like a dream it was;
So like a dream that this should come to pass,
And 'neath her feet the green earth opened not.
But when her breaking heart again waxed hot
With dreadful thoughts and prayers unspeakable
As all their bitter torment on her fell,
When she her own voice heard, nor knew its sound,
And like red flame she saw the trees and ground,
Then first she seemed to know what misery
To helpless folk upon the earth can be.

But while beneath the many moving feet
The small crushed flowers sent up their odour sweet,
Above sat Venus, calm, and very fair,
Her white limbs bared of all her golden hair,
Into her heart all wrath cast back again,
As on the terror and the helpless pain
She gazed with gentle eyes, and unmoved smile;
Such as in Cyprus, the fair blossomed isle,

When on the altar in the summer night
They pile the roses up for her delight,
Men see within their hearts, and long that they
Unto her very body there might pray.
At last to them some dainty sign she made
To hold their cruel hands, and therewith bade
To bear her slave new gained from out her sight
And keep her safely till the morrow's light:
So her across the sunny sward they led
With fainting limbs, and heavy downcast head,
And into some nigh lightless prison cast
To brood alone o'er happy days long past
And all the dreadful times that yet should be.
But she being gone, one moment pensively
The goddess did the distant hills behold,
Then bade her girls bind up her hair of gold,
And veil her breast, the very forge of love,
With raiment that no earthly shuttle wove,
And 'gainst the hard earth arm her lovely feet:
Then she went forth, some shepherd king to meet
Deep in the hollow of a shaded vale,
To make his woes a long-enduring tale.

But over Psyche, hapless and forlorn,
Unseen the sun rose on the morrow morn,
Nor knew she aught about the death of night
Until her gaoler's torches filled with light
The dreary place, blinding her unused eyes,
And she their voices heard that bade her rise;
She did their bidding, yet grown faint and pale
She shrank away and strove her arms to veil
In her gown's bosom, and to hide from them
Her little feet within her garment's hem;
But mocking her, they brought her thence away,
And led her forth into the light of day,
And brought her to a marble cloister fair
Where sat the queen on her adornéd chair,
But she, as down the sun-streaked place they came,
Cried out, "Haste! ye, who lead my grief and shame."
And when she stood before her trembling, said,
"Although within a palace thou wast bred
Yet dost thou carry but a slavish heart,
And fitting is it thou shouldst learn thy part,
And know the state whereunto thou art brought;
Now, heed what yesterday thy folly taught,
And set thyself to-day my will to do;
Ho ye, bring that which I commanded you."

Then forth came two, and each upon her back
Bore up with pain a huge half-bursten sack,
Which, setting down, they opened on the floor,

And from their hempen mouths a stream did pour
Of mingled seeds, and grain, peas, pulse, and wheat,
Poppies and millet, and coriander sweet,
And many another brought from far-off lands,
Which mingling more with swift and ready hands
They piled into a heap confused and great.
And then said Venus, rising from her seat,
"Slave, here I leave thee, but before the night
These mingled seeds thy hands shall set aright,
All laid in heaps, each after its own kind,
And if in any heap I chance to find
An alien seed; thou knowest since yesterday
How disobedient slaves the forfeit pay."
Therewith she turned and left the palace fair
And from its outskirts rose into the air,
And flew until beneath her lay the sea,
Then, looking on its green waves lovingly,
Somewhat she dropped, and low adown she flew
Until she reached the temple that she knew
Within a sunny bay of her fair isle.

But Psyche sadly labouring all the while
With hopeless heart felt the swift hours go by,
And knowing well what bitter mockery
Lay in that task, yet did she what she might
That something should be finished ere the night,
And she a little mercy yet might ask;
But the first hours of that long feverish task
Passed amid mocks; for oft the damsels came
About her, and made merry with her shame,
And laughed to see her trembling eagerness,
And how, with some small lappet of her dress,
She winnowed out the wheat, and how she bent
Over the millet, hopelessly intent;
And how she guarded well some tiny heap
But just begun, from their long raiments' sweep;
And how herself, with girt gown, carefully
She went betwixt the heaps that 'gan to lie
Along the floor; though they were small enow,
When shadows lengthened and the sun was low;
But at the last these left her labouring,
Not daring now to weep, lest some small thing
Should 'scape her blinded eyes, and soon far off
She heard the echoes of their careless scoff.
Longer the shades grew, quicker sank the sun,
Until at last the day was well-nigh done,
And every minute did she think to hear
The fair Queen's dreaded footsteps drawing near;
But Love, that moves the earth, and skies, and sea,
Beheld his old love in her misery,
And wrapped her heart in sudden gentle sleep;

And meanwhile caused unnumbered ants to creep
About her, and they wrought so busily
That all, ere sundown, was as it should be,
And homeward went again the kingless folk.
Bewildered with her joy again she woke,
But scarce had time the unseen hands to bless,
That thus had helped her utter feebleness,
Ere Venus came, fresh from the watery way,
Panting with all the pleasure of the day;
But when she saw the ordered heaps, her smile
Faded away, she cried out, "Base and vile
Thou art indeed, this labour fitteth thee;
But now I know thy feigned simplicity,
Thine inward cunning, therefore hope no more,
Since thou art furnished well with hidden lore,
To 'scape thy due reward, if any day
Without some task accomplished, pass away!"
So with a frown she passed on, muttering,
"Nought have I done, to-morrow a new thing."

So the next morning Psyche did they lead
Unto a terrace o'er a flowery mead,
Where Venus sat, hid from the young sun's rays,
Upon the fairest of all summer days;
She pointed o'er the meads as they drew nigh,
And said, "See how that stream goes glittering by,
And on its banks my golden sheep now pass,
Cropping sweet mouthfuls of the flowery grass;
If thou, O cunning slave, to-day art fain
To save thyself from well-remembered pain,
Put forth a little of thy hidden skill,
And with their golden fleece thy bosom fill;
Yet make no haste, but ere the sun is down
Cast it before my feet from out thy gown;
Surely thy labour is but light to-day."
Then sadly went poor Psyche on her way,
Wondering wherein the snare lay, for she knew
No easy thing it was she had to do;
Nor had she failed indeed to note the smile
Wherewith the goddess praised her for the guile
That she, unhappy, lacked so utterly.
Amidst these thoughts she crossed the flowery lea,
And came unto the glittering river's side;
And, seeing it was neither deep nor wide,
She drew her sandals off, and to the knee
Girt up her gown, and by a willow-tree
Went down into the water, and but sank
Up to mid-leg therein; but from the bank
She scarce had gone three steps, before a voice
Called out to her, "Stay, Psyche, and rejoice
That I am here to help thee, a poor reed,

The soother of the loving hearts that bleed,
The pourer forth of notes, that oft have made
The weak man strong, and the rash man afraid.
"Sweet child, when by me now thy dear foot trod,
I knew thee for the loved one of our god;
Then prithee take my counsel in good part;
Go to the shore again, and rest thine heart
In sleep awhile, until the sun get low,
And then across the river shalt thou go
And find these evil creatures sleeping fast,
And on the bushes whereby they have passed
Much golden wool; take what seems good to thee,
And ere the sun sets go back easily.
But if within that mead thou sett'st thy feet
While yet they wake, an ill death shalt thou meet,
For they are of a cursed man-hating race,
Bred by a giant in a lightless place."
But at these words soft tears filled Psyche's eyes
As hope of love within her heart did rise;
And when she saw she was not helpless yet
Her old desire she would not quite forget;
But turning back, upon the bank she lay
In happy dreams till nigh the end of day;
Then did she cross and gather of the wool,
And with her bosom and her gown-skirt full
Came back to Venus at the sun-setting;
But she afar off saw it glistering
And cried aloud, "Go, take the slave away,
And keep her safe for yet another day,
And on the morning will I think again
Of some fresh task, since with so little pain
She doeth what the gods find hard enow;
For since the winds were pleased this waif to blow
Unto my door, a fool I were indeed,
If I should fail to use her for my need."
So her they led away from that bright sun,
Now scarce more hopeful that the task was done,
Since by those bitter words she knew full well
Another tale the coming day would tell.

But the next morn upon a turret high,
Where the wind kissed her raiment lovingly,
Stood Venus waiting her; and when she came
She said, "O slave, thy city's very shame,
Lift up thy cunning eyes, and looking hence
Shalt thou behold betwixt these battlements,
A black and barren mountain set aloof
From the green hills, shaped like a palace roof.
Ten leagues from hence it lieth, toward the north,
And from its rocks a fountain welleth forth,
Black like itself, and floweth down its side,

And in a while part into Styx doth glide,
And part into Cocytus runs away,
Now coming thither by the end of day,
Fill me this ewer from out the awful stream;
Such task a sorceress like thee will deem
A little matter; bring it not to pass,
And if thou be not made of steel or brass,
To-morrow shalt thou find the bitterest day
Thou yet hast known, and all be sport and play
To what thy heart in that hour shall endure
Behold, I swear it, and my word is sure!"
She turned therewith to go down toward the sea,
To meet her lover, who from Thessaly
Was come from some well-foughten field of war.
But Psyche, wandering wearily afar,
Reached the bare foot of that black rock at last,
And sat there grieving for the happy past,
For surely now, she thought, no help could be,
She had but reached the final misery,
Nor had she any counsel but to weep.
For not alone the place was very steep,
And craggy beyond measure, but she knew
What well it was that she was driven to,
The dreadful water that the gods swear by,
For there on either hand, as one draws nigh,
Are long-necked dragons ready for the spring,
And many another monstrous nameless thing,
The very sight of which is well-nigh death;
Then the black water as it goes crieth,
"Fly, wretched one, before you come to die!
Die, wretched man! I will not let you fly!
How have you heart to come before me here?
You have no heart, your life is turned to fear!"
Till the wretch falls adown with whirling brain,
And far below the sharp rocks end his pain.
Well then might Psyche wail her wretched fate,
And strive no more, but sitting weep and wait
Alone in that black land for kindly death,
With weary sobbing, wasting life and breath;
But o'er her head there flew the bird of Jove,
The bearer of his servant, friend of Love,
Who, when he saw her, straightway towards her flew,
And asked her why she wept, and when he knew,
And who she was, he said, "Cease all thy fear,
For to the black waves I thy ewer will bear,
And fill it for thee; but, remember me,
When thou art come unto thy majesty."
Then straight he flew, and through the dragon's wings
Went carelessly, nor feared their clatterings,
But set the ewer, filled, in her right hand,
And on that day saw many another land.

Then Psyche through the night toiled back again,
And as she went, she thought, "Ah! all is vain,
For though once more I just escape indeed,
Yet hath she many another wile at need;
And to these days when I my life first learn,
With unavailing longing shall I turn,
When this that seemeth now so horrible
Shall then seem but the threshold of her hell.
Alas! what shall I do? for even now
In sleep I see her pitiless white brow,
And hear the dreadful sound of her commands,
While with my helpless body and bound hands
I tremble underneath the cruel whips;
And oft for dread of her, with quivering lips
I wake, and waking know the time draws nigh
When nought shall wake me from that misery
Behold, O Love, because of thee I live,
Because of thee, with these things still I strive."

Now with the risen sun her weary feet
The late-strewn roses of the floor did meet
Upon the marble threshold of the place;
But she being brought before the matchless face,
Fresh with the new life of another day,
Beheld her wondering, for the goddess lay
With half-shut eyes upon her golden bed,
And when she entered scarcely turned her head,
But smiling spake, "The gods are good to thee,
Nor shalt thou always be mine enemy;
But one more task I charge thee with to-day,
Now unto Proserpine take thou thy way,
And give this golden casket to her hands,
And pray the fair Queen of the gloomy lands
To fill the void shell with that beauty rare
That long ago as queen did set her there;
Nor needest thou to fail in this new thing,
Who hast to-day the heart and wit to bring
This dreadful water, and return alive;
And, that thou may'st the more in this thing strive,
If thou returnest I will show at last
My kindness unto thee, and all the past
Shalt thou remember as an ugly dream."
And now at first to Psyche did it seem
Her heart was softening to her, and the thought
Swelled her full heart to sobbing, and it brought
Into her yearning eyes half-happy tears:
But on her way cold thoughts and dreadful fears
Rose in her heart, for who indeed could teach
A living soul that dread abode to reach
And yet return? and then once more it seemed

The hope of mercy was but lightly dreamed,
And she remembered that triumphant smile,
And needs must think, "This is the final wile,
Alas! what trouble must a goddess take
So weak a thing as this poor heart to break.
"See now this tower! from off its top will I
Go quick to Proserpine, ah, good to die!
Rather than hear those shameful words again,
And bear that unimaginable pain
Which she has hoarded for to-morrow morn;
Now is the ending of my life forlorn!
O Love, farewell, thou seest all hope is dead,
Thou seest what torments on my wretched head
Thy bitter mother doth not cease to heap;
Farewell, O Love, for thee and life I weep.
Alas, my foolish heart! alas, my sin!
Alas, for all the love I could not win!"

Now was this tower both old enough and grey,
Built by some king forgotten many a day,
And no man dwelt there, now that bitter war
From that bright land had long been driven afar;
There now she entered, trembling and afraid;
But 'neath her doubtful steps the dust long laid
In utter rest, rose up into the air,
And wavered in the wind that down the stair
Rushed to the door; then she drew back a pace,
Moved by the coolness of the lonely place
That for so long had seen no ray of sun.
Then shuddering did she hear these words begun,
Like a wind's moaning voice, "Have thou no fear
The hollow words of one long slain to hear!
Thou livest, and thy hope is not yet dead,
And if thou heedest me, thou well may'st tread
The road to hell, and yet return again.
"For thou must go o'er many a hill and plain
Until to Sparta thou art come at last,
And when the ancient city thou hast passed
A mountain shalt thou reach, that men now call
Mount Tænarus, that riseth like a wall
'Twixt plain and upland, therein shalt thou find
The wide mouth of a cavern huge and blind,
Wherein there cometh never any sun,
Whose dreadful darkness all things living shun;
This shun thou not, but yet take care to have
Three honey-cakes thy soul alive to save,
And in thy mouth a piece of money set,
Then through the dark go boldly, and forget
The stories thou hast heard of death and hell,
And heed my words, and then shall all be well.
"For when thou hast passed through that cavern blind,

A place of dim grey meadows shalt thou find,
Wherethrough to inmost hell a path doth lead,
Which follow thou, with diligence and heed;
For as thou goest there, thou soon shalt see
Two men like peasants loading painfully
A fallen ass; these unto thee will call
To help them, but give thou no heed at all,
But pass them swiftly; and then soon again
Within a shed three crones shalt thou see plain
Busily weaving, who shall bid thee leave
The road and fill their shuttles while they weave,
But slacken not thy steps for all their prayers,
For these are shadows only, and set snares.
"At last thou comest to a water wan,
And at the bank shall be the ferryman
Surly and grey; and when he asketh thee
Of money for thy passage, hastily
Show him thy mouth, and straight from off thy lip
The money he will take, and in his ship
Embark thee and set forward; but beware,
For on thy passage is another snare;
From out the waves a grisly head shall come,
Most like thy father thou hast left at home,
And pray for passage long and piteously,
But on thy life of him have no pity,
Else art thou lost; also thy father lives,
And in the temples of the high gods gives
Great daily gifts for thy returning home.
"When thou unto the other side art come,
A palace shalt thou see of fiery gold,
And by the door thereof shalt thou behold
An ugly triple monster, that shall yell
For thine undoing; now behold him well,
And into each mouth of him cast a cake,
And no more heed of thee then shall he take,
And thou may'st pass into a glorious hall
Where many a wonder hangs upon the wall;
But far more wonderful than anything
The fair slim consort of the gloomy King,
Arrayed all royally shalt thou behold,
Who sitting on a carven throne of gold,
Whene'er thou enterest shall rise up to thee,
And bid thee welcome there most lovingly,
And pray thee on a royal bed to sit,
And share her feast; yet eat thou not of it,
But sitting on the ground eat bread alone,
Then do thy message kneeling by her throne;
And when thou hast the gift, return with speed;
The sleepy dog of thee shall take no heed,
The ferryman shall bear thee on thy way
Without more words, and thou shalt see the day

Unharmed if that dread box thou openest not;
But if thou dost, then death shall be thy lot.

"O beautiful, when safe thou com'st again,
Remember me, who lie here in such pain
Unburied; set me in some tomb of stone.
When thou hast gathered every little bone;
But never shalt thou set thereon a name,
Because my ending was with grief and shame,
Who was a Queen like thee long years agone,
And in this tower so long have lain alone."

Then, pale and full of trouble, Psyche went
Bearing the casket, and her footsteps bent
To Lacedæmon, and thence found her way
To Tænarus, and there the golden day
For that dark cavern did she leave behind;
Then, going boldly through it, did she find
The shadowy meads which that wide way ran through,
Under a seeming sky 'twixt grey and blue;
No wind blew there, there was no bird or tree,
Or beast, and dim grey flowers she did but see
That never faded in that changeless place,
And if she had but seen a living face
Most strange and bright she would have thought it there,
Or if her own face, troubled yet so fair,
The still pools by the road-side could have shown
The dimness of that place she might have known;
But their dull surface cast no image back,
For all but dreams of light that land did lack.
So on she passed, still noting every thing,
Nor yet had she forgotten there to bring
The honey-cakes and money: in a while
She saw those shadows striving hard to pile
The bales upon the ass, and heard them call,
"O woman, help us! for our skill is small
And we are feeble in this place indeed;"
But swiftly did she pass, nor gave them heed,
Though after her from far their cries they sent.
Then a long way adown that road she went,
Not seeing aught, till, as the Shade had said,
She came upon three women in a shed
Busily weaving, who cried, "Daughter, leave
The beaten road a while, and as we weave
Fill thou our shuttles with these endless threads,
For here our eyes are sleepy, and our heads
Are feeble in this miserable place."
But for their words she did but mend her pace,
Although her heart beat quick as she passed by.

Then on she went, until she could espy

The wan, grey river lap the leaden bank
Wherefrom there sprouted sparsely sedges rank,
And there the road had end in that sad boat
Wherein the dead men unto Minos float;
There stood the ferryman, who now, seeing her, said,
"O living soul, that thus among the dead
Hast come, on whatso errand, without fear,
Know thou that penniless none passes here;
Of all the coins that rich men have on earth
To buy the dreadful folly they call mirth,
But one they keep when they have passed the grave
That o'er this stream a passage they may have;
And thou, though living, art but dead to me,
Who here, immortal, see mortality
Pass, stripped of this last thing that men desire
Unto the changeless meads or changeless fire."
Speechless she shewed the money on her lip
Which straight he took, and set her in the ship,
And then the wretched, heavy oars he threw
Into the rowlocks and the flood they drew;
Silent, with eyes that looked beyond her face,
He laboured, and they left the dreary place.
But midmost of that water did arise
A dead man, pale, with ghastly staring eyes
That somewhat like her father still did seem,
But in such wise as figures in a dream;
Then with a lamentable voice it cried,
"O daughter, I am dead, and in this tide
For ever shall I drift, an unnamed thing,
Who was thy father once, a mighty king,
Unless thou take some pity on me now,
And bid the ferryman turn here his prow,
That I with thee to some abode may cross;
And little unto thee will be the loss,
And unto me the gain will be to come
To such a place as I may call a home,
Being now but dead and empty of delight,
And set in this sad place 'twixt dark and light."
Now at these words the tears ran down apace
For memory of the once familiar face,
And those old days, wherein, a little child
'Twixt awe and love beneath those eyes she smiled;
False pity moved her very heart, although
The guile of Venus she failed not to know,
But tighter round the casket clasped her hands,
And shut her eyes, remembering the commands
Of that dead queen: so safe to land she came.

And there in that grey country, like a flame
Before her eyes rose up the house of gold,
And at the gate she met the beast threefold,

Who ran to meet her open-mouthed, but she
Unto his jaws the cakes cast cunningly,
But trembling much; then on the ground he lay
Lolling his heads, and let her go her way;
And so she came into the mighty hall,
And saw those wonders hanging on the wall,
That all with pomegranates was covered o'er
In memory of the meal on that sad shore,
Whereby fair Enna was bewept in vain,
And this became a kingdom and a chain.
But on a throne, the Queen of all the dead
She saw therein with gold-embracéd head,
In royal raiment, beautiful and pale;
Then with slim hands her face did Psyche veil
In worship of her, who said, "Welcome here,
O messenger of Venus! thou art dear
To me thyself indeed, for of thy grace
And loveliness we know e'en in this place;
Rest thee then, fair one, on this royal bed
And with some dainty food shalt thou be fed;
Ho, ye who wait, bring in the tables now!"
Therewith were brought things glorious of show
On cloths and tables royally beseen,
By damsels each one fairer than a queen,
The very latchets of whose shoes were worth
The royal crown of any queen on earth;
But when upon them Psyche looked, she saw
That all these dainty matters without flaw
Were strange of shape and of strange-blended hues
So every cup and plate did she refuse
Those lovely hands brought to her, and she said,
"O Queen, to me amidst my awe and dread
These things are nought, my message is not done,
So let me rest upon this cold grey stone,
And while my eyes no higher than thy feet
Are lifted, eat the food that mortals eat."
Therewith upon the floor she sat her down
And from the folded bosom of her gown
Drew forth her bread and ate, while with cold eyes
Regarding her 'twixt anger and surprise,
The Queen sat silent for awhile, then spoke,
"Why art thou here, wisest of living folk?
Depart in haste, lest thou shouldst come to be
Thyself a helpless thing and shadowy!
Give me the casket then, thou need'st not say
Wherefore thou thus hast passed the awful way;
Bide there, and for thy mistress shalt thou have
The charm that beauty from all change can save."
Then Psyche rose, and from her trembling hand
Gave her the casket, and awhile did stand
Alone within the hall, that changing light

From burning streams, and shadowy waves of night
Made strange and dread, till to her, standing there
The world began to seem no longer fair,
Life no more to be hoped for, but that place
The peaceful goal of all the hurrying race,
The house she must return to on some day.
Then sighing scarcely could she turn away
When with the casket came the Queen once more,
And said, "Haste now to leave this shadowy shore
Before thou changest; even now I see
Thine eyes are growing strange, thou look'st on me
E'en as the linnet looks upon the snake.
Behold, thy wisely-guarded treasure take,
And let thy breath of life no longer move
The shadows with the memories of past love."

But Psyche at that name, with quickened heart
Turned eagerly, and hastened to depart
Bearing that burden, hoping for the day;
Harmless, asleep, the triple monster lay,
The ferryman did set her in his boat
Unquestioned, and together did they float
Over the leaden water back again:
Nor saw she more those women bent with pain
Over their weaving, nor the fallen ass,
But swiftly up the grey road did she pass
And well-nigh now was come into the day
By hollow Tænarus, but o'er the way
The wings of Envy brooded all unseen;
Because indeed the cruel and fair Queen
Knew well how she had sped; so in her breast,
Against the which the dreadful box was pressed,
Grew up at last this foolish, harmful thought.
"Behold how far this beauty I have brought
To give unto my bitter enemy;
Might I not still a very goddess be
If this were mine which goddesses desire,
Yea, what if this hold swift consuming fire,
Why do I think it good for me to live,
That I my body once again may give
Into her cruel hands, come death! come life!
And give me end to all the bitter strife!"
Therewith down by the wayside did she sit
And turned the box round, long regarding it;
But at the last, with trembling hands, undid
The clasp, and fearfully raised up the lid;
But what was there she saw not, for her head
Fell back, and nothing she rememberéd
Of all her life, yet nought of rest she had,
The hope of which makes hapless mortals glad;
For while her limbs were sunk in deadly sleep

Most like to death, over her heart 'gan creep
Ill dreams; so that for fear and great distress
She would have cried, but in her helplessness
Could open not her mouth, or frame a word;
Although the threats of mocking things she heard,
And seemed, amidst new forms of horror bound,
To watch strange endless armies moving round,
With all their sleepless eyes still fixed on her,
Who from that changeless place should never stir.
Moveless she lay, and in that dreadful sleep
Scarce had the strength some few slow tears to weep.

And there she would have lain for evermore,
A marble image on the shadowy shore
In outward seeming, but within oppressed
With torments, knowing neither hope nor rest
But as she lay the Phoenix flew along
Going to Egypt, and knew all her wrong,
And pitied her, beholding her sweet face,
And flew to Love and told him of her case;
And Love, in guerdon of the tale he told,
Changed all the feathers of his neck to gold,
And he flew on to Egypt glad at heart.
But Love himself gat swiftly for his part
To rocky Tænarus, and found her there
Laid half a furlong from the outer air.

But at that sight out burst the smothered flame
Of love, when he remembered all her shame,
The stripes, the labour, and the wretched fear,
And kneeling down he whispered in her ear,
"Rise, Psyche, and be mine for evermore,
For evil is long tarrying on this shore."
Then when she heard him, straightway she arose,
And from her fell the burden of her woes;
And yet her heart within her well-nigh broke,
When she from grief to happiness awoke;
And loud her sobbing was in that grey place,
And with sweet shame she covered up her face.
But her dear hands, all wet with tears, he kissed,
And taking them about each dainty wrist
Drew them away, and in a sweet voice said,
"Raise up again, O Psyche, that dear head,
And of thy simpleness have no more shame;
Thou hast been tried, and cast away all blame
Into the sea of woes that thou didst bear,
The bitter pain, the hopelessness, the fear
Holpen a little, loved with boundless love
Amidst them all, but now the shadows move
Fast toward the west, earth's day is well-nigh done,
One toil thou hast yet; by to-morrow's sun

Kneel the last time before my mother's feet,
Thy task accomplished; and my heart, O sweet,
Shall go with thee to ease thy toilsome way;
Farewell awhile! but that so glorious day
I promised thee of old, now cometh fast,
When even hope thy soul aside shall cast,
Amidst the joy that thou shalt surely win."
So saying, all that sleep he shut within
The dreadful casket, and aloft he flew,
But slowly she unto the cavern drew
Scarce knowing if she dreamed, and so she came
Unto the earth where yet the sun did flame
Low down between the pine-trunks, tall and red,
And with its last beams kissed her golden head.

With what words Love unto the Father prayed
I know not, nor what deeds the balance weighed;
But this I know, that he prayed not in vain,
And Psyche's life the heavenly crown shall gain;
So round about the messenger was sent
To tell immortals of their King's intent,
And bid them gather to the Father's hall.
But while they got them ready at his call,
On through the night was Psyche toiling still,
To whom no pain nor weariness seemed ill
Since now once more she knew herself beloved;
But when the unresting world again had moved
Round into golden day, she came again
To that fair place where she had borne such pain,
And flushed and joyful in despite her fear,
Unto the goddess did she draw anear,
And knelt adown before her golden seat,
Laying the fatal casket at her feet;
Then at the first no word the Sea-born said,
But looked afar over her golden head,
Pondering upon the mighty deeds of fate;
While Psyche still, as one who well may wait,
Knelt, calm and motionless, nor said a word,
But ever thought of her sweet lovesome lord.
At last the Queen said, "Girl, I bid thee rise,
For now hast thou found favour in mine eyes;
And I repent me of the misery
That in this place thou hast endured of me,
Although because of it, thy joy indeed
Shall now be more, that pleasure is thy meed."
Then bending, on the forehead did she kiss
Fair Psyche, who turned red for shame and bliss;
But Venus smiled again on her, and said,
"Go now, and bathe, and be as well arrayed
As thou shouldst be, to sit beside my son;
I think thy life on earth is well-nigh done."

So thence once more was Psyche led away,
And cast into no prison on that day,
But brought unto a bath beset with flowers,
Made dainty with a fount's sweet-smelling showers,
And there being bathed, e'en in such fair attire
As veils the glorious Mother of Desire
Her limbs were veiled, then in the wavering shade,
Amidst the sweetest garden was she laid,
And while the damsels round her watch did keep,
At last she closed her weary eyes in sleep,
And woke no more to earth, for ere the day
Had yet grown late, once more asleep she lay
Within the West Wind's mighty arms, nor woke
Until the light of heaven upon her broke,
And on her trembling lips she felt the kiss
Of very Love, and mortal yet, for bliss
Must fall a-weeping. O for me! that I,
Who late have told her woe and misery,
Must leave untold the joy unspeakable
That on her tender wounded spirit fell!
Alas! I try to think of it in vain,
My lyre is but attuned to tears and pain,
How shall I sing the never-ending day?

Led by the hand of Love she took her way
Unto a vale beset with heavenly trees,
Where all the gathered gods and goddesses
Abode her coming; but when Psyche saw
The Father's face, she fainting with her awe
Had fallen, but that Love's arm held her up.
Then brought the cup-bearer a golden cup,
And gently set it in her slender hand,
And while in dread and wonder she did stand,
The Father's awful voice smote on her ear,
"Drink now, O beautiful, and have no fear!
For with this draught shalt thou be born again.
And live for ever free from care and pain."

Then, pale as privet, took she heart to drink,
And therewithal most strange new thoughts did think,
And unknown feelings seized her, and there came
Sudden remembrance, vivid as a flame,
Of everything that she had done on earth,
Although it all seemed changed in weight and worth,
Small things becoming great, and great things small;
And godlike pity touched her therewithal
For her old self, for sons of men that die;
And that sweet new-born immortality
Now with full love her rested spirit fed.

Then in that concourse did she lift her head,
And stood at last a very goddess there,
And all cried out at seeing her grown so fair.

So while in heaven quick passed the time away,
About the ending of that lovely day,
Bright shone the low sun over all the earth
For joy of such a wonderful new birth.

Or e'er his tale was done, night held the earth;
Yea, the brown bird grown bold, as sounds of mirth
Grew faint and scanty, now his tale had done,
And by his mate abode the next day's sun;
And in those old hearts did the story move
Remembrance of the mighty deeds of love,
And with these thoughts did hopes of life arise,
Till tears unseen were in their ancient eyes,
And in their yearning hearts unspoken prayers,
And idle seemed the world with all its cares.

Few words they said; the balmy odorous wind
Wandered about, some resting-place to find;
The young leaves rustled 'neath its gentle breath,
And here and there some blossom burst his sheath,
Adding unnoticed fragrance to the night;
But, as they pondered, a new golden light
Streamed over the green garden, and they heard
Sweet voices sing some ancient poet's word
In praise of May, and then in sight there came
The minstrels' figures underneath the flame
Of scented torches passing 'twixt the trees,
And soon the dusky hall grew bright with these,
And therewithal they put all thought away,
And midst the tinkling harps drank deep to May.

Through many changes had the May-tide passed,
The hope of summer oft had been o'ercast,
Ere midst the gardens they once more were met;
But now the full-leaved trees might well forget
The changeful agony of doubtful spring,
For summer pregnant with so many a thing
Was at the door; right hot had been the day
Which they amid the trees had passed away,
And now betwixt the tulip beds they went
Unto the hall, and thoughts of days long spent
Gathered about them, as some blossom's smell
Unto their hearts familiar tales did tell.
But when they well were settled in the hall,
And now behind the trees the sun 'gan fall,
And they as yet no history had heard,
Laurence, the Swabian priest, took up the word,

And said, "Ye know from what has gone before,
That in my youth I followed mystic lore,
And many books I read in seeking it,
And through my memory this same eve doth flit
A certain tale I found in one of these,
Long ere mine eyes had looked upon the seas;
It made me shudder in the times gone by,
When I believed in many a mystery
I thought divine, that now I think, forsooth,
Men's own fears made, to fill the place of truth
Within their foolish hearts; short is the tale,
And therefore will the better now avail
To fill the space before the night comes on,
And unto rest once more the world is won.

THE WRITING ON THE IMAGE

ARGUMENT

How on an image that stood anciently in Rome were written certain words, which none understood, until a Scholar, coming there, knew their meaning, and thereby discovered great marvels, but withal died miserably.

In half-forgotten days of old,
As by our fathers we were told,
Within the town of Rome there stood
An image cut of cornel wood,
And on the upraised hand of it
Men might behold these letters writ:
"PERCUTE HIC:" which is to say,
In that tongue that we speak to-day,
"Strike here!" nor yet did any know
The cause why this was written so.

Thus in the middle of the square,
In the hot sun and summer air,
The snow-drift and the driving rain,
That image stood, with little pain,
For twice a hundred years and ten;
While many a band of striving men
Were driven betwixt woe and mirth
Swiftly across the weary earth,
From nothing unto dark nothing:
And many an emperor and king,
Passing with glory or with shame,
Left little record of his name,
And no remembrance of the face
Once watched with awe for gifts or grace

Fear little, then, I counsel you,
What any son of man can do;
Because a log of wood will last
While many a life of man goes past,
And all is over in short space.

Now so it chanced that to this place
There came a man of Sicily,
Who when the image he did see,
Knew full well who, in days of yore,
Had set it there; for much strange lore,
In Egypt and in Babylon,
This man with painful toil had won;
And many secret things could do;
So verily full well he knew
That master of all sorcery
Who wrought the thing in days gone by,
And doubted not that some great spell
It guarded, but could nowise tell
What it might be. So, day by day,
Still would he loiter on the way,
And watch the image carefully,
Well mocked of many a passer-by.
And on a day he stood and gazed
Upon the slender finger, raised
Against a doubtful cloudy sky,
Nigh noontide; and thought, "Certainly
The master who made thee so fair
By wondrous art, had not stopped there,
But made thee speak, had he not thought
That thereby evil might be brought
Upon his spell." But as he spoke,
From out a cloud the noon sun broke
With watery light, and shadows cold:
Then did the Scholar well behold
How, from that finger carved to tell
Those words, a short black shadow fell
Upon a certain spot of ground,
And thereon, looking all around
And seeing none heeding, went straightway
Whereas the finger's shadow lay,
And with his knife about the place
A little circle did he trace;
Then home he turned with throbbing head,
And forthright gat him to his bed,
And slept until the night was late
And few men stirred from gate to gate.
So when at midnight he did wake,
Pickaxe and shovel did he take,
And, going to that now silent square,
He found the mark his knife made there,

And quietly with many a stroke
The pavement of the place he broke:
And so, the stones being set apart,
He 'gan to dig with beating heart,
And from the hole in haste he cast
The marl and gravel; till at last,
Full shoulder high, his arms were jarred,
For suddenly his spade struck hard
With clang against some metal thing:
And soon he found a brazen ring,
All green with rust, twisted, and great
As a man's wrist, set in a plate
Of copper, wrought all curiously
With words unknown though plain to see,
Spite of the rust; and flowering trees,
And beasts, and wicked images,
Whereat he shuddered: for he knew
What ill things he might come to do,
If he should still take part with these
And that Great Master strive to please.
But small time had he then to stand
And think, so straight he set his hand
Unto the ring, but where he thought
That by main strength it must be brought
From out its place, lo! easily
It came away, and let him see
A winding staircase wrought of stone,
Wherethrough the new-come wind did moan.
Then thought he, "If I come alive
From out this place well shall I thrive,
For I may look here certainly
The treasures of a king to see,
A mightier man than men are now.
So in few days what man shall know
The needy Scholar, seeing me
Great in the place where great men be,
The richest man in all the land?
Beside the best then shall I stand,
And some unheard-of palace have;
And if my soul I may not save
In heaven, yet here in all men's eyes
Will I make some sweet paradise,
With marble cloisters, and with trees
And bubbling wells, and fantasies,
And things all men deem strange and rare,
And crowds of women kind and fair,
That I may see, if so I please,
Laid on the flowers, or mid the trees
With half-clad bodies wandering.
There, dwelling happier than the king,
What lovely days may yet be mine!

How shall I live with love and wine,
And music, till I come to die!
And then - Who knoweth certainly
What haps to us when we are dead?
Truly I think by likelihead
Nought haps to us of good or bad;
Therefore on earth will I be glad
A short space, free from hope or fear;
And fearless will I enter here
And meet my fate, whatso it be."

Now on his back a bag had he,
To bear what treasure he might win,
And therewith now did he begin
To go adown the winding stair;
And found the walls all painted fair
With images of many a thing,
Warrior and priest, and queen and king,
But nothing knew what they might be.
Which things full clearly could he see,
For lamps were hung up here and there
Of strange device, but wrought right fair,
And pleasant savour came from them.
At last a curtain, on whose hem
Unknown words in red gold were writ,
He reached, and softly raising it
Stepped back, for now did he behold
A goodly hall hung round with gold,
And at the upper end could see
Sitting, a glorious company:
Therefore he trembled, thinking well
They were no men, but fiends of hell.
But while he waited, trembling sore,
And doubtful of his late-earned lore,
A cold blast of the outer air
Blew out the lamps upon the stair
And all was dark behind him; then
Did he fear less to face those men
Than, turning round, to leave them there
While he went groping up the stair.
Yea, since he heard no cry or call
Or any speech from them at all,
He doubted they were images
Set there some dying king to please
By that Great Master of the art;
Therefore at last with stouter heart
He raised the cloth and entered in
In hope that happy life to win,
And drawing nigher did behold
That these were bodies dead and cold
Attired in full royal guise,

And wrought by art in such a wise
That living they all seemed to be,
Whose very eyes he well could see,
That now beheld not foul or fair,
Shining as though alive they were.
And midmost of that company
An ancient king that man could see,
A mighty man, whose beard of grey
A foot over his gold gown lay;
And next beside him sat his queen
Who in a flowery gown of green
And golden mantle well was clad,
And on her neck a collar had
Too heavy for her dainty breast;
Her loins by such a belt were prest
That whoso in his treasury
Held that alone, a king might be.
On either side of these, a lord
Stood heedfully before the board,
And in their hands held bread and wine
For service; behind these did shine
The armour of the guards, and then
The well-attiréd serving-men,
The minstrels clad in raiment meet;
And over against the royal seat
Was hung a lamp, although no flame
Was burning there, but there was set
Within its open golden fret
A huge carbuncle, red and bright;
Wherefrom there shone forth such a light
That great hall was as clear by it,
As though by wax it had been lit,
As some great church at Easter-tide.
Now set a little way aside,
Six paces from the daïs stood
An image made of brass and wood,
In likeness of a full-armed knight
Who pointed 'gainst the ruddy light
A huge shaft ready in a bow.
Pondering how he could come to know
What all these marvellous matters meant,
About the hall the Scholar went,
Trembling, though nothing moved as yet;
And for awhile did he forget
The longings that had brought him there
In wondering at these marvels fair;
And still for fear he doubted much
One jewel of their robes to touch.

But as about the hall he passed
He grew more used to them at last,

And thought, "Swiftly the time goes by,
And now no doubt the day draws nigh
Folk will be stirring: by my head
A fool I am to fear the dead,
Who have seen living things enow,
Whose very names no man can know,
Whose shapes brave men might well affright
More than the lion in the night
Wandering for food;" therewith he drew
Unto those royal corpses two,
That on dead brows still wore the crown;
And midst the golden cups set down
The rugged wallet from his back,
Patched of strong leather, brown and black.
Then, opening wide its mouth, took up
From off the board, a golden cup
The King's dead hand was laid upon,
Whose unmoved eyes upon him shone
And recked no more of that last shame
Than if he were the beggar lame,
Who in old days was wont to wait
For a dog's meal beside the gate.
Of which shame nought our man did reck.
But laid his hand upon the neck
Of the slim Queen, and thence undid
The jewelled collar, that straight slid
Down her smooth bosom to the board.
And when these matters he had stored
Safe in his sack, with both their crowns,
The jewelled parts of their rich gowns,
Their shoes and belts, brooches and rings,
And cleared the board of all rich things,
He staggered with them down the hall.
But as he went his eyes did fall
Upon a wonderful green stone,
Upon the hall-floor laid alone;
He said, "Though thou art not so great
To add by much unto the weight
Of this my sack indeed, yet thou,
Certes, would make me rich enow,
That verily with thee I might
Wage one-half of the world to fight
The other half of it, and I
The lord of all the world might die;
I will not leave thee;" therewithal
He knelt down midmost of the hall,
Thinking it would come easily
Into his hand; but when that he
Gat hold of it, full fast it stack,
So fuming, down he laid his sack,
And with both hands pulled lustily,

But as he strained, he cast his eye
Back to the daïs; there he saw
The bowman image 'gin to draw
The mighty bowstring to his ear,
So, shrieking out aloud for fear,
Of that rich stone he loosed his hold
And catching up his bag of gold,
Gat to his feet: but ere he stood
The evil thing of brass and wood
Up to his ear the notches drew;
And clanging, forth the arrow flew,
And midmost of the carbuncle
Clanging again, the forked barbs fell,
And all was dark as pitch straightway.

So there until the judgment day
Shall come and find his bones laid low
And raise them up for weal or woe,
This man must bide; cast down he lay
While all his past life day by day
In one short moment he could see
Drawn out before him, while that he
In terror by that fatal stone
Was laid, and scarcely dared to moan.
But in a while his hope returned,
And then, though nothing he discerned,
He gat him up upon his feet,
And all about the walls he beat
To find some token of the door,
But never could he find it more,
For by some dreadful sorcery
All was sealed close as it might be
And midst the marvels of that hall
This scholar found the end of all.

But in the town on that same night,
An hour before the dawn of light,
Such storm upon the place there fell,
That not the oldest man could tell
Of such another: and thereby
The image was burnt utterly,
Being stricken from the clouds above;
And folk deemed that same bolt did move
The pavement where that wretched one
Unto his foredoomed fate had gone,
Because the plate was set again
Into its place, and the great rain
Washed the earth down, and sorcery
Had hid the place where it did lie.
So soon the stones were set all straight,
But yet the folk, afraid of fate,

Where once the man of cornel wood
Through many a year of bad and good
Had kept his place, set up alone
Great Jove himself, cut in white stone,
But thickly overlaid with gold.
"Which," saith my tale, "you may behold
Unto this day, although indeed
Some Lord or other, being in need,
Took every ounce of gold away."
But now, this tale in some past day
Being writ, I warrant all is gone,
Both gold and weather-beaten stone.

Be merry, masters, while ye may,
For men much quicker pass away.

They praised the tale, and for awhile they talked
Of other tales of treasure-seekers balked,
And shame and loss for men insatiate stored,
Nitocris' tomb, the Niblungs' fatal hoard,
The serpent-guarded treasures of the dead;
Then of how men would be rememberéd
When they are gone; and more than one could tell
Of what unhappy things therefrom befell;
Or how by folly men have gained a name;
A name indeed, not hallowed by the fame
Of any deeds remembered: and some thought,
"Strange hopes and fears for what shall be but nought
To dead men! better it would be to give
What things they may, while on the earth they live
Unto the earth, and from the bounteous earth
To take their pay of sorrow or of mirth,
Hatred or love, and get them on their way;
And let the teeming earth fresh troubles make
For other men, and ever for their sake
Use what they left, when they are gone from it."

But while amid such musings they did sit,
Dark night being come, men lighted up the hall,
And the chief man for minstrelsy did call,
And other talk their dull thoughts chased away,
Nor did they part till night was mixed with day.

JUNE

O June, O June, that we desired so,
Wilt thou not make us happy on this day?
Across the river thy soft breezes blow
Sweet with the scent of beanfields far away,

Above our heads rustle the aspens grey,
Calm is the sky with harmless clouds beset,
No thought of storm the morning vexes yet.

See, we have left our hopes and fears behind
To give our very hearts up unto thee;
What better place than this then could we find
By this sweet stream that knows not of the sea,
That guesses not the city's misery,
This little stream whose hamlets scarce have names,
This far-off, lonely mother of the Thames?

Here then, O June, thy kindness will we take;
And if indeed but pensive men we seem,
What should we do? thou wouldst not have us wake
From out the arms of this rare happy dream
And wish to leave the murmur of the stream,
The rustling boughs, the twitter of the birds,
And all thy thousand peaceful happy words.

Now in the early June they deemed it good
That they should go unto a house that stood
On their chief river, so upon a day
With favouring wind and tide they took their way
Up the fair stream; most lovely was the time
Even amidst the days of that fair clime,
And still the wanderers thought about their lives,
And that desire that rippling water gives
To youthful hearts to wander anywhere.
So midst sweet sights and sounds a house most fair
They came to, set upon the river side
Where kindly folk their coming did abide;
There they took land, and in the lime-trees' shade
Beneath the trees they found the fair feast laid,
And sat, well pleased; but when the water-hen
Had got at last to think them harmless men,
And they with rest, and pleasure, and old wine,
Began to feel immortal and divine,
An elder spoke, "O gentle friends, the day
Amid such calm delight now slips away,
And ye yourselves are grown so bright and glad
I care not if I tell you something sad;
Sad, though the life I tell you of passed by,
Unstained by sordid strife or misery;
Sad, because though a glorious end it tells,
Yet on the end of glorious life it dwells,
And striving through all things to reach the best
Upon no midway happiness will rest."

ARGUMENT

Admetus, King of Pheræ in Thessaly, received unwittingly Apollo as his servant, by the help of whom he won to wife Alcestis, daughter of Pelias: afterwards too, as in other things, so principally in this, Apollo gave him help, that when he came to die, he obtained of the Fates for him, that if another would die willingly in his stead, then he should live still; and when to every one else this seemed impossible, Alcestis gave her life for her husband's.

Midst sunny grass-clad meads that slope adown
To lake Boebeis stands an ancient town,
Where dwelt of old a lord of Thessaly,
The son of Pheres and fair Clymene,
Who had to name Admetus: long ago
The dwellers by the lake have ceased to know
His name, because the world grows old, but then
He was accounted great among great men;
Young, strong, and godlike, lacking nought at all
Of gifts that unto royal men might fall
In those old simple days, before men went
To gather unseen harm and discontent,
Along with all the alien merchandise
That rich folk need, too restless to be wise.

Now on the fairest of all autumn eves,
When midst the dusty, crumpled, dying leaves
The black grapes showed, and every press and vat
Was newly scoured, this King Admetus sat
Among his people, wearied in such wise
By hopeful toil as makes a paradise
Of the rich earth; for light and far away
Seemed all the labour of the coming day,
And no man wished for more than then he had,
Nor with another's mourning was made glad.
There in the pillared porch, their supper done,
They watched the fair departing of the sun;
The while the soft-eyed well-girt maidens poured
The joy of life from out the jars long stored
Deep in the earth, while little like a king,
As we call kings, but glad with everything,
The wise Thessalian sat and blessed his life,
So free from sickening fear and foolish strife.
But midst the joy of this festivity,
Turning aside he saw a man draw nigh,
Along the dusty grey vine-bordered road
That had its ending at his fair abode;
He seemed e'en from afar to set his face
Unto the King's adornéd reverend place,
And like a traveller went he wearily,
And yet as one who seems his rest to see.

A staff he bore, but nowise was he bent
With scrip or wallet; so withal he went
Straight to the King's high seat, and standing near,
Seemed a stout youth and noble, free from fear,
But peaceful and unarmed; and though ill clad,
And though the dust of that hot land he had
Upon his limbs and face, as fair was he
As any king's son you might lightly see,
Grey-eyed and crisp-haired, beautiful of limb,
And no ill eye the women cast on him.
But kneeling now, and stretching forth his hand,
He said, "O thou, the king of this fair land,
Unto a banished man some shelter give,
And help me with thy goods that I may live:
Thou hast good store, Admetus, yet may I,
Who kneel before thee now in misery,
Give thee more gifts before the end shall come
Than all thou hast laid safely in thine home."
"Rise up, and be my guest," Admetus said,
"I need no gifts for this poor gift of bread,
The land is wide, and bountiful enow.
What thou canst do, to-morrow thou shalt show,
And be my man, perchance; but this night rest
Not questioned more than any passing guest.
Yea, even if a great king thou hast spilt,
Thou shall not answer aught but as thou wilt."
Then the man rose and said, "O King, indeed
Of thine awarded silence have I need,
Nameless I am, nameless what I have done
Must be through many circles of the sun.
But for to-morrow, let me rather tell
On this same eve what things I can do well,
And let me put mine hand in thine and swear
To serve thee faithfully a changing year;
Nor think the woods of Ossa hold one beast
That of thy tenderest yearling shall make feast,
Whiles that I guard thy flocks, and thou shalt bear
Thy troubles easier when thou com'st to hear
The music I can make. Let these thy men
Witness against me if I fail thee, when
War falls upon thy lovely land and thee."
Then the King smiled, and said, "So let it be,
Well shalt thou serve me, doing far less than this,
Nor for thy service due gifts shalt thou miss:
Behold I take thy faith with thy right hand,
Be thou true man unto this guarded land.
Ho ye! take this my guest, find raiment meet
Wherewith to clothe him; bathe his wearied feet,
And bring him back beside my throne to feast."
But to himself he said, "I am the least
Of all Thessalians if this man was born

In any earthly dwelling more forlorn
Than a king's palace."
Then a damsel slim
Led him inside, nought loth to go with him,
And when the cloud of steam had curled to meet
Within the brass his wearied dusty feet,
She from a carved press brought him linen fair,
And a new-woven coat a king might wear,
And so being clad he came unto the feast,
But as he came again, all people ceased
What talk they held soever, for they thought
A very god among them had been brought;
And doubly glad the king Admetus was
At what that dying eve had brought to pass,
And bade him sit by him and feast his fill.
So there they sat till all the world was still,
And 'twixt the pillars their red torches' shine
Held forth unto the night a joyous sign.

So henceforth did this man at Pheræ dwell,
And what he set his hand to wrought right well,
And won much praise and love in everything,
And came to rule all herdsmen of the King;
But for two things in chief his fame did grow;
And first that he was better with the bow
Than any 'twixt Olympus and the sea,
And then that sweet, heart-piercing melody
He drew out from the rigid-seeming lyre,
And made the circle round the winter fire
More like to heaven than gardens of the May.
So many a heavy thought he chased away
From the King's heart, and softened many a hate,
And choked the spring of many a harsh debate;
And, taught by wounds, the snatchers of the wolds
Lurked round the gates of less well-guarded folds.
Therefore Admetus loved him, yet withal,
Strange doubts and fears upon his heart did fall;
For morns there were when he the man would meet,
His hair wreathed round with bay and blossoms sweet,
Gazing distraught into the brightening east,
Nor taking heed of either man or beast,
Or anything that was upon the earth.
Or sometimes, midst the hottest of the mirth,
Within the King's hall, would he seem to wake
As from a dream, and his stringed tortoise take
And strike the cords unbidden, till the hall
Filled with the glorious sound from wall to wall,
Trembled and seemed as it would melt away,
And sunken down the faces weeping lay
That erewhile laughed the loudest; only he
Stood upright, looking forward steadily

With sparkling eyes as one who cannot weep,
Until the storm of music sank to sleep.

But this thing seemed the doubtfullest of all
Unto the King, that should there chance to fall
A festal day, and folk did sacrifice
Unto the gods, ever by some device
The man would be away: yet with all this
His presence doubled all Admetus' bliss,
And happy in all things he seemed to live,
And great gifts to his herdsman did he give.
But now the year came round again to spring,
And southward to Iolchos went the King;
For there did Pelias hold a sacrifice
Unto the gods, and put forth things of price
For men to strive for in the people's sight;
So on a morn of April, fresh and bright,
Admetus shook the golden-studded reins,
And soon from windings of the sweet-banked lanes
The south wind blew the sound of hoof and wheel,
Clatter of brazen shields and clink of steel
Unto the herdsman's ears, who stood awhile
Hearkening the echoes with a godlike smile,
Then slowly gat him foldwards, murmuring,
"Fair music for the wooing of a King."
But in six days again Admetus came,
With no lost labour or dishonoured name;
A scarlet cloak upon his back he bare
A gold crown on his head, a falchion fair
Girt to his side; behind him four white steeds,
Whose dams had fed full in Nisæan meads;
All prizes that his valiant hands had won
Within the guarded lists of Tyro's son.
Yet midst the sound of joyous minstrelsy
No joyous man in truth he seemed to be;
So that folk looking on him said, "Behold,
The wise King will not show himself too bold
Amidst his greatness: the gods too are great,
And who can tell the dreadful ways of fate?"
Howe'er it was, he gat him through the town,
And midst their shouts at last he lighted down
At his own house, and held high feast that night;
And yet by seeming had but small delight
In aught that any man could do or say:
And on the morrow, just at dawn of day,
Rose up and clad himself, and took his spear.
And in the fresh and blossom-scented air
Went wandering till he reach Boebeis' shore;
Yet by his troubled face set little store
By all the songs of birds and scent of flowers;
Yea, rather unto him the fragrant hours

Were grown but dull and empty of delight.
So going, at the last he came in sight
Of his new herdsman, who that morning lay
Close by the white sand of a little bay
The teeming ripple of Boebeis lapped;
There he in cloak of white-wooled sheepskin wrapped
Against the cold dew, free from trouble sang,
The while the heifers' bells about him rang
And mingled with the sweet soft-throated birds
And bright fresh ripple: listen, then, these words
Will tell the tale of his felicity,
Halting and void of music though they be.

SONG

O Dwellers on the lovely earth,
Why will ye break your rest and mirth
To weary us with fruitless prayer;
Why will ye toil and take such care
For children's children yet unborn,
And garner store of strife and scorn
To gain a scarce-remembered name,
Cumbered with lies and soiled with shame?
And if the gods care not for you,
What is this folly ye must do
To win some mortal's feeble heart?
O fools! when each man plays his part,
And heeds his fellow little more
Than these blue waves that kiss the shore
Take heed of how the daisies grow.
O fools! and if ye could but know
How fair a world to you is given.

O brooder on the hills of heaven,
When for my sin thou drav'st me forth,
Hadst thou forgot what this was worth,
Thine own hand had made? The tears of men,
The death of threescore years and ten,
The trembling of the timorous race
Had these things so bedimmed the place
Thine own hand made, thou couldst not know
To what a heaven the earth might grow
If fear beneath the earth were laid,
If hope failed not, nor love decayed.

He stopped, for he beheld his wandering lord,
Who, drawing near, heard little of his word,
And noted less; for in that haggard mood
Nought could he do but o'er his sorrows brood,
Whate'er they were, but now being come anigh,
He lifted up his drawn face suddenly,

And as the singer gat him to his feet,
His eyes Admetus' troubled eyes did meet,
As with some speech he now seemed labouring,
Which from his heart his lips refused to bring.
Then spoke the herdsman, "Master, what is this,
That thou, returned with honour to the bliss,
The gods have given thee here, still makest show
To be some wretch bent with the weight of woe?
What wilt thou have? What help there is in me
Is wholly thine, for in felicity
Within thine house thou still hast let me live,
Nor grudged most noble gifts to me to give."

"Yea," said Admetus, "thou canst help indeed,
But as the spring shower helps the unsown mead.
Yet listen: at Iolchos the first day
Unto Diana's house I took my way,
Where all men gathered ere the games began,
There, at the right side of the royal man,
Who rules Iolchos, did his daughter stand,
Who with a suppliant bough in her right hand
Headed the band of maidens; but to me
More than a goddess did she seem to be,
Nor fit to die; and therewithal I thought
That we had all been thither called for nought
But that her bridegroom Pelias might choose,
And with that thought desire did I let loose,
And striving not with Love, I gazed my fill,
As one who will not fear the coming ill:
All, foolish were mine eyes, foolish my heart,
To strive in such a marvel to have part!
What god shall wed her rather? no more fear
Than vexes Pallas vexed her forehead clear,
Faith shone from out her eyes, and on her lips
Unknown love trembled; the Phoenician ships
Within their dark holds nought so precious bring
As her soft golden hair, no daintiest thing
I ever saw was half so wisely wrought
As was her rosy ear; beyond all thought,
All words to tell of, her veiled body showed,
As, by the image of the Three-formed bowed,
She laid her offering down; then I drawn near
The murmuring of her gentle voice could hear,
As waking one hears music in the morn,
Ere yet the fair June sun is fully born;
And sweeter than the roses fresh with dew
Sweet odours floated round me, as she drew
Some golden thing from out her balmy breast
With her right hand, the while her left hand pressed
The hidden wonders of her girdlestead;
And when abashed I sank adown my head,

Dreading the god of Love, my eyes must meet
The happy bands about her perfect feet.
"What more? thou know'st perchance what thing love is?
Kindness, and hot desire, and rage, and bliss,
None first a moment; but before that day
No love I knew but what might pass away
When hot desire was changed to certainty,
Or not abide much longer; e'en such stings
Had smitten me, as the first warm day brings
When March is dying; but now half a god
The crowded way unto the lists I trod,
Yet hopeless as a vanquished god at whiles,
And hideous seemed the laughter and the smiles,
And idle talk about me on the way.
"But none could stand before me on that day,
I was as god-possessed, not knowing how
The King had brought her forth but for a show,
To make his glory greater through the land:
Therefore at last victorious did I stand
Among my peers, nor yet one well-known name
Had gathered any honour from my shame.
For there indeed both men of Thessaly,
Oetolians, Thebans, dwellers by the sea,
And folk of Attica and Argolis,
Arcadian woodmen, islanders, whose bliss
Is to be tossed about from wave to wave,
All these at last to me the honour gave,
Nor did they grudge it: yea, and one man said,
A wise Thessalian with a snowy head,
And voice grown thin with age, 'O Pelias,
Surely to thee no evil thing it was
That to thy house this rich Thessalian
Should come, to prove himself a valiant man
Amongst these heroes; for if I be wise
By dint of many years, with wistful eyes
Doth he behold thy daughter, this fair maid;
And surely, if the matter were well weighed,
Good were it both for thee and for the land
That he should take the damsel by the hand
And lead her hence, for ye near neighbours dwell;
What sayest thou, King, have I said ill or well?'
"With that must I, a fool, stand forth and ask
If yet there lay before me some great task
That I must do ere I the maid should wed,
But Pelias, looking on us, smiled and said,
'O neighbour of Larissa, and thou too,
O King Admetus, this may seem to you
A little matter; yea, and for my part
E'en such a marriage would make glad my heart;
But we the blood of Salmoneus who share
With godlike gifts great burdens also bear,

Nor is this maid without them, for the day
On which her maiden zone she puts away
Shall be her death-day, if she wed with one
By whom this marvellous thing may not be done,
For in the traces neither must steeds paw
Before my threshold, or white oxen draw
The wain that comes my maid to take from me,
Far other beasts that day her slaves must be:
The yellow lion 'neath the lash must roar,
And by his side unscared, the forest boar
Toil at the draught: what sayest thou then hereto,
O lord of Pheræ, wilt thou come to woo
In such a chariot, and win endless fame,
Or turn thine eyes elsewhere with little shame?'
"What answered I? O herdsman, I was mad
With sweet love and the triumph I had had.
I took my father's ring from off my hand,
And said, 'O heroes of the Grecian land,
Be witnesses that on my father's name
For this man's promise, do I take the shame
Of this deed undone, if I fail herein;
Fear not, O Pelias, but that I shall win
This ring from thee, when I shall come again
Through fair Iolchos, driving that strange wain.
Else by this token, thou, O King, shalt have
Pheræ my home, while on the tumbling wave
A hollow ship my sad abode shall be.'
"So driven by some hostile deity,
Such words I said, and with my gifts hard won,
But little valued now, set out upon
My homeward way: but nearer as I drew
To mine abode, and ever fainter grew
In my weak heart the image of my love,
In vain with fear my boastful folly strove;
For I remembered that no god I was
Though I had chanced my fellows to surpass;
And I began to mind me in a while
What murmur rose, with what a mocking smile
Pelias stretched out his hand to take the ring.
Made by my drunkard's gift now twice a king:
And when unto my palace-door I came
I had awakened fully to my shame;
For certainly no help is left to me,
But I must get me down unto the sea
And build a keel, and whatso things I may
Set in her hold, and cross the watery way
Whither Jove bids, and the rough winds may blow
Unto a land where none my folly know,
And there begin a weary life anew."

Eager and bright the herdsman's visage grew

The while this tale was told, and at the end
He said, "Admetus, I thy life may mend,
And thou at lovely Pheræ still may dwell;
Wait for ten days, and then may all be well,
And thou to fetch thy maiden home may go,
And to the King thy team unheard-of show.
And if not, then make ready for the sea
Nor will I fail indeed to go with thee,
And 'twixt the halyards and the ashen oar
Finish the service well begun ashore;
But meanwhile do I bid thee hope the best;
And take another herdsman for the rest,
For unto Ossa must I go alone
To do a deed not easy to be done."

Then springing up he took his spear and bow
And northward by the lake-shore 'gan to go;
But the King gazed upon him as he went,
Then, sighing, turned about, and homeward bent
His lingering steps, and hope began to spring
Within his heart, for some betokening
He seemed about the herdsman now to see
Of one from mortal cares and troubles free.
And so midst hopes and fears day followed day,
Until at last upon his bed he lay
When the grey, creeping dawn had now begun
To make the wide world ready for the sun
On the tenth day: sleepless had been the night
And now in that first hour of gathering light
For weariness he slept, and dreamed that he
Stood by the border of a fair, calm sea
At point to go a-shipboard, and to leave
Whatever from his sire he did receive
Of land or kingship; and withal he dreamed
That through the cordage a bright light there gleamed
Far off within the east; and nowise sad
He felt at leaving all he might have had,
But rather as a man who goes to see
Some heritage expected patiently.
But when he moved to leave the firm fixed shore,
The windless sea rose high and 'gan to roar,
And from the gangway thrust the ship aside,
Until he hung over a chasm wide
Vocal with furious waves, yet had no fear
For all the varied tumult he might hear,
But slowly woke up to the morning light
That to his eyes seemed past all memory bright,
And then strange sounds he heard, whereat his heart
Woke up to joyous life with one glad start,
And nigh his bed he saw the herdsman stand,
Holding a long white staff in his right hand,

Carved with strange figures; and withal he said,
"Awake, Admetus! loiter not a-bed,
But haste thee to bring home thy promised bride,
For now an ivory chariot waits outside,
Yoked to such beasts as Pelias bade thee bring;
Whose guidance thou shalt find an easy thing,
If in thine hands thou holdest still this rod,
Whereon are carved the names of every god
That rules the fertile earth; but having come
Unto King Pelias' well-adornéd home,
Abide not long, but take the royal maid,
And let her dowry in thy wain be laid,
Of silver and fine cloth and unmixed gold,
For this indeed will Pelias not withhold
When he shall see thee like a very god.
Then let thy beasts, ruled by this carven rod,
Turn round to Pheræ; yet must thou abide
Before thou comest to the streamlet's side
That feed its dykes; there, by the little wood
Wherein unto Diana men shed blood,
Will I await thee, and thou shalt descend
And hand-in-hand afoot through Pheræ wend;
And yet I bid thee, this night let thy bride
Apart among the womenfolk abide;
That on the morrow thou with sacrifice
For these strange deeds may pay a fitting price."

But as he spoke with something like to awe,
His eyes and much-changed face Admetus saw,
And voiceless like a slave his words obeyed;
For rising up no more delay he made,
But took the staff and gained the palace-door
Where stood the beasts, whose mingled whine and roar
Had wrought his dream; there two and two they stood,
Thinking, it might be, of the tangled wood,
And all the joys of the food-hiding trees,
But harmless as their painted images
'Neath some dread spell; then, leaping up, he took
The reins in hand and the bossed leather shook,
And no delay the conquered beasts durst make
But drew, not silent; and folk just awake
When he went by, as though a god they saw,
Fell on their knees, and maidens come to draw
Fresh water from the fount sank trembling down,
And silence held the babbling wakened town.
So 'twixt the dewy hedges did he wend,
And still their noise afar the beasts did send,
His strange victorious advent to proclaim,
Till to Iolchos at the last he came,
And drew anigh the gates, whence in affright
The guards fled, helpless at the wondrous sight;

And through the town news of the coming spread
Of some great god so that the scared priests led
Pale suppliants forth; who, in unmeet attire
And hastily-caught boughs and smouldering fire
Within their censers, in the market-place
Awaited him with many an upturned face,
Trembling with fear of that unnamed new god;
But through the midst of them his lions trod
With noiseless feet, nor noted aught their prey,
And the boars' hooves went pattering on the way,
While from their churning tusks the white foam flew
As raging, helpless, in the trace they drew.
But Pelias, knowing all the work of fate,
Sat in his brazen-pillared porch to wait
The coming of the King; the while the maid
In her fair marriage garments was arrayed,
And from strong places of his treasury
Men brought fine scarlet from the Syrian sea,
And works of brass, and ivory, and gold;
But when the strange yoked beasts he did behold
Come through the press of people terrified,
Then he arose and o'er the clamour cried,
"Hail, thou, who like a very god art come
To bring great honour to my damsel's home;"
And when Admetus tightened rein before
The gleaming, brazen-wrought, half-opened door.
He cried to Pelias, "Hail, to thee, O King;
Let me behold once more my father's ring,
Let me behold the prize that I have won,
Mine eyes are wearying now to look upon."
"Fear not," he said, "the Fates are satisfied;
Yet wilt thou not descend and here abide,
Doing me honour till the next bright morn
Has dried the dew upon the new-sprung corn,
That we in turn may give the honour due
To such a man that such a thing can do,
And unto all the gods may sacrifice?"
"Nay," said Admetus, "if thou call'st me wise,
And like a very god thou dost me deem,
Shall I abide the ending of the dream
And so gain nothing? nay, let me be glad
That I at least one godlike hour have had
At whatsoever time I come to die,
That I may mock the world that passes by,
And yet forgets it." Saying this, indeed,
Of Pelias did he seem to take small heed,
But spoke as one unto himself may speak,
And still the half-shut door his eyes did seek,
Wherethrough from distant rooms sweet music came,
Setting his over-strainéd heart a-flame,
Because amidst the Lydian flutes he thought

From place to place his love the maidens brought.
Then Pelias said, "What can I give to thee
Who fail'st so little of divinity?
Yet let my slaves lay these poor gifts within
Thy chariot, while my daughter strives to win
The favour of the spirits of this place,
Since from their altars she must turn her face
For ever now; hearken, her flutes I hear,
From the last chapel doth she draw anear."
Then by Admetus' feet the folk 'gan pile
The precious things, but he no less the while
Stared at the door ajar, and thought it long
Ere with the flutes mingled the maidens' song,
And both grew louder, and the scarce-seen floor
Was fluttering with white raiment, and the door
By slender fingers was set open wide,
And midst her damsels he beheld the bride
Ungirt, with hair unbound and garlanded:
Then Pelias took her slender hand and said,
"Daughter, this is the man that takes from thee
Thy curse midst women, think no more to be
Childless, unloved, and knowing little bliss;
But now behold how like a god he is,
And yet with what prayers for the love of thee
He must have wearied some divinity,
And therefore in thine inmost heart be glad
That thou 'mongst women such a man hast had."
Then she with wondering eyes that strange team saw
A moment, then as one with gathering awe
Might turn from Jove's bird unto very Jove,
So did she raise her grey eyes to her love,
But to her brow the blood rose therewithal,
And she must tremble, such a look did fall
Upon her faithful eyes, that none the less
Would falter aught, for all her shamefastness,
But rather to her lover's hungry eyes
Gave back a tender look of glad surprise,
Wherein love's flame began to flicker now.
Withal, her father kissed her on the brow,
And said, "O daughter, take this royal ring,
And set it on the finger of the King,
And come not back; and thou, Admetus, pour
This wine to Jove before my open door,
And glad at heart take back thine own with thee."
Then with that word Alcestis silently,
And with no look cast back, and ring in hand,
Went forth, and soon beside her love did stand
Nor on his finger failed to set the ring;
And then a golden cup the city's King
Gave to him, and he poured and said, "O thou,
From whatsoever place thou lookest now,

What prayers, what gifts unto thee shall I give
That we a little time with love may live?
A little time of love, then fall asleep
Together, while the crown of love we keep."
So spake he, and his strange beasts turned about,
And heeded not the people's wavering shout
That from their old fear and new pleasure sprung,
Nor noted aught of what the damsels sung,
Or of the flowers that after them they cast,
But like a dream the guarded city passed,
And 'twixt the song of birds and blossoms' scent
It seemed for many hundred years they went,
Though short the way was unto Pheræ's gates;
Time they forgat, and gods, and men, and fates,
However nigh unto their hearts they were;
The woodland boars, the yellow lords of fear
No more seemed strange to them, but all the earth
With all its changing sorrow and wild mirth
In that fair hour seemed new-born to the twain,
Grief seemed a play forgot, a pageant vain,
A picture painted, who knows where or when,
With soulless images of restless men;
For every thought but love was now gone by,
And they forgot that they should ever die.

But when they came anigh the sacred wood,
There, biding them, Admetus' herdsman stood,
At sight of whom those yoke-fellows unchecked
Stopped dead and little of Admetus recked
Who now, as one from dreams not yet awake,
Drew back his love and did his wain forsake,
And gave the carven rod and guiding bands
Into the waiting herdsman's outstretched hands,
But when he would have thanked him for the thing
That he had done, his speechless tongue must cling
Unto his mouth, and why he could not tell.
But the man said, "No words! thou hast done well
To me, as I to thee; the day may come
When thou shalt ask me for a fitting home,
Nor shalt thou ask in vain; but hasten now,
And to thine house this royal maiden show,
Then give her to thy women for this night.
But when thou wakest up to thy delight
To-morrow, do all things that should be done,
Nor of the gods, forget thou any one,
And on the next day will I come again
To tend thy flocks upon the grassy plain.
"But now depart, and from thine home send here
Chariot and horse, these gifts of thine to bear
Unto thine house, and going, look not back
Lest many a wished-for thing thou com'st to lack."

Then hand in hand together, up the road
The lovers passed unto the King's abode,
And as they went, the whining snort and roar
From the yoked beasts they heard break out once more
And then die off, as they were led away,
But whether to some place lit up by day,
Or, 'neath the earth, they knew not, for the twain
Went hastening on, nor once looked back again.
But soon the minstrels met them, and a band
Of white-robed damsels flowery boughs in hand,
To bid them welcome to that pleasant place.
Then they, rejoicing much, in no long space
Came to the brazen-pillared porch, whereon
From 'twixt the passes of the hills yet shone
The dying sun; and there she stood awhile
Without the threshold, a faint tender smile
Trembling upon her lips 'twixt love and shame,
Until each side of her a maiden came
And raised her in their arms, that her fair feet
The polished brazen threshold might not meet,
And in Admetus' house she stood at last.
But to the women's chamber straight she passed
Bepraised of all, and so the wakeful night
Lonely the lovers passed e'en as they might.
But the next day with many a sacrifice,
Admetus wrought, for such a well-won prize,
A life so blest, the gods to satisfy,
And many a matchless beast that day did die
Upon the altars; nought unlucky seemed
To be amid the joyous crowd that gleamed
With gold and precious things, and only this
Seemed wanting to the King of Pheræ's bliss,
That all these pageants should be soon past by,
And hid by night the fair spring blossoms lie.

Yet on the morrow-morn Admetus came,
A haggard man oppressed with grief and shame
Unto the spot beside Boebeis' shore
Whereby he met his herdsman once before,
And there again he found him flushed and glad,
And from the babbling water newly clad,
Then he with downcast eyes these words began,
"O thou, whatso thy name is, god or man,
Hearken to me; meseemeth of thy deed
Some dread immortal taketh angry heed.
"Last night the height of my desire seemed won,
All day my weary eyes had watched the sun
Rise up and sink, and now was come the night
When I should be alone with my delight;
Silent the house was now from floor to roof,
And in the well-hung chambers, far aloof,

The feasters lay; the moon was in the sky,
The soft spring wind was wafting lovingly
Across the gardens fresh scents to my sweet,
As, troubled with the sound of my own feet,
I passed betwixt the pillars, whose long shade
Black on the white red-veinéd floor was laid:
So happy was I that the briar-rose,
Rustling outside within the flowery close,
Seemed but Love's odorous wing, too real all seemed
For such a joy as I had never dreamed.
"Why do I linger, as I lingered not
In that fair hour, now ne'er to be forgot
While my life lasts? Upon the gilded door
I laid my hand; I stood upon the floor
Of the bride-chamber, and I saw the bride,
Lovelier than any dream, stand by the side
Of the gold bed, with hands that hid her face:
One cry of joy I gave, and then the place
Seemed changed to hell as in a hideous dream.
"Still did the painted silver pillars gleam
Betwixt the scented torches and the moon;
Still did the garden shed its odorous boon
Upon the night; still did the nightingale
Unto his brooding mate tell all his tale:
But, risen 'twixt my waiting love and me,
As soundless as the dread eternity,
Sprung up from nothing, could mine eyes behold
A huge dull-gleaming dreadful coil that rolled
In changing circles on the pavement fair.
Then for the sword that was no longer there
My hand sank to my side; around I gazed,
And 'twixt the coils I met her grey eyes, glazed
With sudden horror most unspeakable;
And when mine own upon no weapon fell,
For what should weapons do in such a place,
Unto the dragon's head I set my face,
And raised bare hands against him, but a cry
Burst on mine ears of utmost agony
That nailed me there, and she cried out to me,
'O get thee hence; alas, I cannot flee!
They coil about me now, my lips to kiss.
O love, why hast thou brought me unto this?'
"Alas, my shame! trembling, away I slunk,
Yet turning saw the fearful coil had sunk
To whence it came, my love's limbs freed I saw,
And a long breath at first I heard her draw
As one redeemed, then heard the hard sobs come,
And wailings for her new accurséd home.
But there outside across the door I lay,
Like a scourged hound, until the dawn of day;
And as her gentle breathing then I heard

As though she slept, before the earliest bird
Began his song, I wandered forth to seek
Thee, O strange man, e'en as thou seest me, weak
With all the torment of the night, and shamed
With such a shame as never shall be named
To aught but thee. Yea, yea, and why to thee
Perchance this ends all thou wilt do for me?
What then, and have I not a cure for that?
Lo, yonder is a rock where I have sat
Full many an hour while yet my life was life,
With hopes of all the coming wonder rife.
No sword hangs by my side, no god will turn
This cloudless hazy blue to black, and burn
My useless body with his lightning flash;
But the white waves above my bones may wash,
And when old chronicles our house shall name
They may leave out the letters and the shame,
That make Admetus, once a king of men
And how could I be worse or better then?"

As one who notes a curious instrument
Working against the maker's own intent,
The herdsman eyed his wan face silently,
And smiling for a while, and then said he,
"Admetus, thou, in spite of all I said,
Hast drawn this evil thing upon thine head,
Forgetting her who erewhile laid the curse
Upon the maiden, so for fear of worse
Go back again; for fair-limbed Artemis
Now bars the sweet attainment of thy bliss;
So taking heart, yet make no more delay
But worship her upon this very day,
Nor spare for aught, and of thy trouble make
No semblance unto any for her sake;
And thick upon the fair bride-chamber floor
Strew dittany, and on each side the door
Hang up such poppy-leaves as spring may yield;
And for the rest, myself may be a shield
Against her wrath, nay, be thou not too bold
To ask me that which may not now be told.
Yea, even what thou deemest, hide it deep
Within thine heart, and let thy wonder sleep,
For surely thou shalt one day know my name,
When the time comes again that autumn's flame
Is dying off the vine-boughs, overturned,
Stripped of their wealth. But now let gifts be burned
To her I told thee of, and in three days
Shall I by many hard and rugged ways
Have come to thee again to bring thee peace.
Go, the sun rises and the shades decrease."
Then, thoughtfully, Admetus gat him back,

Nor did the altars of the Huntress lack
The fattest of the flocks upon that day.
But when night came, in arms Admetus lay
Across the threshold of the bride-chamber,
And nought amiss that night he noted there,
But durst not enter, though about the door
Young poppy-leaves were twined, and on the floor,
Not flowered as yet with downy leaves and grey,
Fresh dittany beloved of wild goats lay.
But when the whole three days and nights were done,
The herdsman came with rising of the sun,
And said, "Admetus, now rejoice again,
Thy prayers and offerings have not been in vain,
And thou at last mayst come unto thy bliss;
And if thou askest for a sign of this,
Take thou this token; make good haste to rise,
And get unto the garden-close that lies
Below these windows sweet with greenery,
And in the midst a marvel shalt thou see,
Three white, black-hearted poppies blossoming,
Though this is but the middle of the spring."
Nor was it otherwise than he had said,
And on that day with joy the twain were wed,
And 'gan to lead a life of great delight;
But the strange woeful history of that night,
The monstrous car, the promise to the King,
All these through weary hours of chiselling
Were wrought in stone, and in Diana's wall
Set up, a joy and witness unto all.
But neither so would wingéd time abide,
The changing year came round to autumn-tide,
Until at last the day was fully come
When the strange guest first reached Admetus' home.
Then, when the sun was reddening to its end,
He to Admetus' brazen porch did wend,
Whom there he found feathering a poplar dart,
Then said he, "King, the time has come to part.
Come forth, for I have that to give thine ear
No man upon the earth but thou must hear."
Then rose the King, and with a troubled look
His well-steeled spear within his hand he took,
And by his herdsman silently he went
As to a peakéd hill his steps he bent,
Nor did the parting servant speak one word,
As up they climbed, unto his silent lord,
Till from the top he turned about his head
From all the glory of the gold light, shed
Upon the hill-top by the setting sun,
For now indeed the day was well-nigh done,
And all the eastern vale was grey and cold;
But when Admetus he did now behold,

Panting beside him from the steep ascent,
One much-changed godlike look on him he bent.
And said, "O mortal, listen, for I see
Thou deemest somewhat of what is in me;
Fear not! I love thee, even as I can
Who cannot feel the woes and ways of man
In spite of this my seeming, for indeed
Now thou beholdest Jove's immortal seed,
And what my name is I would tell thee now,
If men who dwell upon the earth as thou
Could hear the name and live; but on the earth.
With strange melodious stories of my birth,
Phoebus men call me, and Latona's son.
"And now my servitude with thee is done,
And I shall leave thee toiling on thine earth,
This handful, that within its little girth
Holds that which moves you so, O men that die;
Behold, to-day thou hast felicity,
But the times change, and I can see a day
When all thine happiness shall fade away;
And yet be merry, strive not with the end,
Thou canst not change it; for the rest, a friend
This year has won thee who shall never fail;
But now indeed, for nought will it avail
To say what I may have in store for thee,
Of gifts that men desire; let these things be,
And live thy life, till death itself shall come,
And turn to nought the storehouse of thine home,
Then think of me; these feathered shafts behold,
That here have been the terror of the wold,
Take these, and count them still the best of all
Thine envied wealth, and when on thee shall fall
By any way the worst extremity,
Call upon me before thou com'st to die,
And lay these shafts with incense on a fire,
That thou mayst gain thine uttermost desire."

He ceased, but ere the golden tongue was still
An odorous mist had stolen up the hill,
And to Admetus first the god grew dim,
And then was but a lovely voice to him,
And then at last the sun had sunk to rest,
And a fresh wind blew lightly from the west
Over the hill-top, and no soul was there;
But the sad dying autumn field-flowers fair,
Rustled dry leaves about the windy place,
Where even now had been the godlike face,
And in their midst the brass-bound quiver lay.
Then, going further westward, far away,
He saw the gleaming of Peneus wan
'Neath the white sky, but never any man,

Except a grey-haired shepherd driving down
From off the long slopes to his fold-yard brown
His woolly sheep, with whom a maiden went,
Singing for labour done and sweet content
Of coming rest; with that he turned again,
And took the shafts up, never sped in vain,
And came unto his house most deep in thought
Of all the things the varied year had brought.

Thenceforth in bliss and honour day by day
His measured span of sweet life wore away.
A happy man he was; no vain desire
Of foolish fame had set his heart a-fire;
No care he had the ancient bounds to change,
Nor yet for him must idle soldiers range
From place to place about the burdened land,
Or thick upon the ruined cornfields stand;
For him no trumpets blessed the bitter war,
Wherein the right and wrong so mingled are,
That hardly can the man of single heart
Amid the sickening turmoil choose his part;
For him sufficed the changes of the year,
The god-sent terror was enough of fear
For him; enough the battle with the earth,
The autumn triumph over drought and dearth.
Better to him than wolf-moved battered shields,
O'er poor dead corpses, seemed the stubble-fields
Danced down beneath the moon, until the night
Grew dreamy with a shadowy sweet delight,
And with the high-risen moon came pensive thought,
And men in love's despite must grow distraught
And loiter in the dance, and maidens drop
Their gathered raiment, and the fifer stop
His dancing notes the pensive drone that chid,
And as they wander to their dwellings, hid
By the black shadowed trees, faint melody,
Mournful and sweet, their soft good-night must be.
Far better spoil the gathering vat bore in
Unto the pressing shed, than midst the din
Of falling houses in war's waggon lies
Besmeared with redder stains than Tyrian dyes;
Or when the temple of the sea-born one
With glittering crowns and gallant raiment shone,
Fairer the maidens seemed by no chain bound,
But such as amorous arms might cast around
Their lovely bodies, than the wretched band
Who midst the shipmen by the gangway stand;
Each lonely in her speechless misery,
And thinking of the worse time that shall be,
When midst of folk who scarce can speak her name,
She bears the uttermost of toil and shame.

Better to him seemed that victorious crown,
That midst the reverent silence of the town
He oft would set upon some singer's brow
Than was the conqueror's diadem, blest now
By lying priests, soon, bent and bloody, hung
Within the thorn by linnets well besung,
Who think but little of the corpse beneath,
Though ancient lands have trembled at his breath.
But to this King, fair Ceres' gifts, the days
Whereon men sung in flushed Lyæus' praise
Tales of old time, the bloodless sacrifice
Unto the goddess of the downcast eyes
And soft persuading lips, the ringing lyre
Unto the bearer of the holy fire
Who once had been amongst them, things like these
Seemed meet to him men's yearning to appease,
These were the triumphs of the peaceful king.

And so, betwixt seed-time and harvesting,
With little fear his life must pass away;
And for the rest, he, from the self-same day
That the god left him, seemed to have some share
In that same godhead he had harboured there:
In all things grew his wisdom and his wealth,
And folk beholding the fair state and health
Wherein his land was, said, that now at last
A fragment of the Golden Age was cast
Over the place, for there was no debate,
And men forgot the very name of hate.
Nor failed the love of her he erst had won
To hold his heart as still the years wore on,
And she, no whit less fair than on the day
When from Iolchos first she passed away,
Did all his will as though he were a god,
And loving still, the downward way she trod.
Honour and love, plenty and peace, he had;
Nor lacked for aught that makes a wise man glad,
That makes him like a rich well-honoured guest
Scarce sorry when the time comes, for the rest,
That at the end perforce must bow his head.
And yet, was death not much rememberéd,
As still with happy men the manner is?
Or, was he not so pleased with this world's bliss,
As to be sorry when the time should come
When but his name should hold his ancient home
While he dwelt nowhere? either way indeed,
Will be enough for most men's daily need,
And with calm faces they may watch the world,
And note men's lives hither and thither hurled,
As folk may watch the unfolding of a play
Nor this, nor that was King Admetus' way,

For neither midst the sweetness of his life
Did he forget the ending of the strife,
Nor yet for heavy thoughts of passing pain
Did all his life seem lost to him or vain,
A wasteful jest of Jove, an empty dream;
Rather before him did a vague hope gleam,
That made him a great-hearted man and wise,
Who saw the deeds of men with far-seeing eyes,
And dealt them pitying justice still, as though
The inmost heart of each man he did know;
This hope it was, and not his kingly place
That made men's hearts rejoice to see his face
Rise in the council hall; through this, men felt
That in their midst a son of man there dwelt
Like and unlike them, and their friend through all;
And still as time went on, the more would fall
This glory on the King's belovéd head,
And round his life fresh hope and fear were shed.

Yet at the last his good days passed away,
And sick upon his bed Admetus lay,
'Twixt him and death nought but a lessening veil
Of hasty minutes, yet did hope not fail,
Nor did bewildering fear torment him then,
But still as ever, all the ways of men
Seemed dear to him: but he, while yet his breath
Still held the gateway 'gainst the arms of death,
Turned to his wife, who, bowed beside the bed,
Wept for his love, and dying goodlihead,
And bade her put all folk from out the room,
Then going to the treasury's rich gloom
To bear the arrows forth, the Lycian's gift.
So she, amidst her blinding tears, made shift
To find laid in the inmost treasury
Those shafts, and brought them unto him, but he,
Beholding them, beheld therewith his life,
Both that now past, with many marvels rife,
And that which he had hoped he yet should see.
Then spoke he faintly, "Love, 'twixt thee and me
A film has come, and I am failing fast:
And now our ancient happy life is past;
For either this is death's dividing hand,
And all is done, or if the shadowy land
I yet escape, full surely if I live
The god with life some other gift will give,
And change me unto thee: e'en at this tide
Like a dead man among you all I bide,
Until I once again behold my guest,
And he has given me either life or rest:
Alas, my love! that thy too loving heart
Nor with my life or death can have a part.

O cruel words! yet death is cruel too:
Stoop down and kiss me, for I yearn for you
E'en as the autumn yearneth for the sun."
"O love, a little time we have been one,
And if we now are twain weep not therefore;
For many a man on earth desireth sore
To have some mate upon the toilsome road,
Some sharer of his still increasing load,
And yet for all his longing and his pain
His troubled heart must seek for love in vain,
And till he dies still must he be alone
But now, although our love indeed is gone,
Yet to this land as thou art leal and true
Set now thine hand to what I bid thee do,
Because I may not die; rake up the brands
Upon the hearth, and from these trembling hands
Cast incense thereon, and upon them lay
These shafts, the relics of a happier day,
Then watch with me; perchance I may not die,
Though the supremest hour now draws anigh
Of life or death, O thou who madest me,
The only thing on earth alike to thee,
Why must I be unlike to thee in this?
Consider, if thou dost not do amiss
To slay the only thing that feareth death
Or knows its name, of all things drawing breath
Upon the earth: see now for no short hour,
For no half-halting death, to reach me slower
Than other men, I pray thee, what avail
To add some trickling grains unto the tale
Soon told, of minutes thou dost snatch away
From out the midst of that unending day
Wherein thou dwellest? rather grant me this
To right me wherein thou hast done amiss,
And give me life like thine for evermore."

So murmured he, contending very sore
Against the coming death; but she meanwhile
Faint with consuming love, made haste to pile
The brands upon the hearth, and thereon cast
Sweet incense, and the feathered shafts at last;
Then, trembling, back unto the bed she crept,
And lay down by his side, and no more wept,
Nay scarce could think of death for very love
That in her faithful heart for ever strove
'Gainst fear and grief: but now the incense-cloud
The old familiar chamber did enshroud,
And on the very verge of death drawn close
Wrapt both their weary souls in strange repose,
That through sweet sleep sent kindly images
Of simple things; and in the midst of these,

Whether it were but parcel of their dream,
Or that they woke to it as some might deem,
I know not, but the door was opened wide,
And the King's name a voice long silent cried,
And Phoebus on the very threshold trod,
And yet in nothing liker to a god
Than when he ruled Admetus' herds, for he
Still wore the homespun coat men used to see
Among the heifers in the summer morn,
And round about him hung the herdsman's horn,
And in his hand he bore the herdsman's spear
And cornel bow, the prowling dog-wolfs fear,
Though empty of its shafts the quiver was.
He to the middle of the room did pass,
And said, "Admetus, neither all for nought
My coming to thee is, nor have I brought
Good tidings to thee; poor man, thou shalt live
If any soul for thee sweet life will give
Enforced by none: for such a sacrifice
Alone the fates can deem a fitting price
For thy redemption; in no battle-field,
Maddened by hope of glory life to yield,
To give it up to heal no city's shame
In hope of gaining long-enduring fame;
For whoso dieth for thee must believe
That thou with shame that last gift wilt receive,
And strive henceforward with forgetfulness
The honied draught of thy new life to bless.
Nay, and moreover such a glorious heart
Who loves thee well enough with life to part
But for thy love, with life must lose love too,
Which e'en when wrapped about in weeds of woe
Is godlike life indeed to such an one.
"And now behold, three days ere life is done
Do the Fates give thee, and I, even I,
Upon thy life have shed felicity
And given thee love of men, that they in turn
With fervent love of thy dear love might burn.
The people love thee and thy silk-clad breast,
Thine open doors have given thee better rest
Than woods of spears or hills of walls might do.
And even now in wakefulness and woe
The city lies, calling to mind thy love
Wearying with ceaseless prayers the gods above.
But thou, thine heart is wise enough to know
That they no whit from their decrees will go."

So saying, swiftly from the room he passed;
But on the world no look Admetus cast,
But peacefully turned round unto the wall
As one who knows that quick death must befall:

For in his heart he thought, "Indeed too well
I know what men are, this strange tale to tell
To those that live with me: yea, they will weep,
And o'er my tomb most solemn days will keep,
And in great chronicles will write my name,
Telling to many an age my deeds and fame.
For living men such things as this desire,
And by such ways will they appease the fire
Of love and grief: but when death comes to stare
Full in men's faces, and the truth lays bare,
How can we then have wish for anything,
But unto life that gives us all to cling?"
So said he, and with closed eyes did await,
Sleeping or waking, the decrees of fate.

But now Alcestis rose, and by the bed
She stood, with wild thoughts passing through her head.
Dried were her tears, her troubled heart and sore
Throbbed with the anguish of her love no more.
A strange look on the dying man she cast,
Then covered up her face and said, "O past!
Past the sweet times that I remember well!
Alas, that such a tale my heart can tell!
Ah, how I trusted him! what love was mine!
How sweet to feel his arms about me twine,
And my heart beat with his! what wealth of bliss
To hear his praises! all to come to this,
That now I durst not look upon his face,
Lest in my heart that other thing have place.
That which I knew not, that which men call hate.
"O me, the bitterness of God and fate!
A little time ago we two were one;
I had not lost him though his life was done,
For still was he in me, but now alone
Through the thick darkness must my soul make moan,
For I must die: how can I live to bear
An empty heart about, the nurse of fear?
How can I live to die some other tide,
And, dying, hear my loveless name outcried
About the portals of that weary land
Whereby my shadowy feet should come to stand.
"Alcestis! O Alcestis, hadst thou known
That thou one day shouldst thus be left alone,
How hadst thou borne a living soul to love!
Hadst thou not rather lifted hands to Jove,
To turn thine heart to stone, thy front to brass,
That through this wondrous world thy soul might pass,
Well pleased and careless, as Diana goes
Through the thick woods, all pitiless of those
Her shafts smite down? Alas! how could it be
Can a god give a god's delights to thee?

Nay rather, Jove, but give me once again,
If for one moment only, that sweet pain
The love I had while still I thought to live!
Ah! wilt thou not, since unto thee I give
My life, my hope? But thou, I come to thee.
Thou sleepest: O wake not, nor speak to me
In silence let my last hour pass away,
And men forget my bitter feeble day."

With that she laid her down upon the bed,
And nestling to him, kissed his weary head,
And laid his wasted hand upon her breast,
Yet woke him not; and silence and deep rest
Fell on that chamber. The night wore away
Mid gusts of wailing wind, the twilight grey
Stole o'er the sea, and wrought his wondrous change
On things unseen by night, by day not strange,
But now half seen and strange; then came the sun,
And therewithal the silent world and dun
Waking, waxed many-coloured, full of sound,
As men again their heap of troubles found,
And woke up to their joy or misery.
But there, unmoved by aught, those twain did lie,
Until Admetus' ancient nurse drew near
Unto the open door, and full of fear
Beheld them moving not, and as folk dead;
Then, trembling with her eagerness and dread,
She cried, "Admetus! art thou dead indeed?
Alcestis! livest thou my words to heed?
Alas, alas, for this Thessalian folk!"
But with her piercing cry the King awoke,
And round about him wildly 'gan to stare,
As a bewildered man who knows not where
He has awakened: but not thin or wan
His face was now, as of a dying man,
But fresh and ruddy; and his eyes shone clear,
As of a man who much of life may bear.
And at the first, but joy and great surprise
Shone out from those awakened, new-healed eyes;
But as for something more at last he yearned,
Unto his love with troubled brow he turned,
For still she seemed to sleep: alas, alas!
Her lonely shadow even now did pass
Along the changeless fields, oft looking back,
As though it yet had thought of some great lack.
And here, the hand just fallen from off his breast
Was cold; and cold the bosom his hand pressed.
And even as the colour lit the day
The colour from her lips had waned away;
Yet still, as though that longed-for happiness
Had come again her faithful heart to bless,

Those white lips smiled, unwrinkled was her brow,
But of her eyes no secrets might he know,
For, hidden by the lids of ivory,
Had they beheld that death a-drawing nigh.

Then o'er her dead corpse King Admetus hung,
Such sorrow in his heart as his faint tongue
Refused to utter; yet the just-past night
But dimly he remembered, and the sight
Of the Far-darter, and the dreadful word
That seemed to cleave all hope as with a sword:
Yet stronger in his heart a knowledge grew,
That nought it was but her fond heart and true
That all the marvel for his love had wrought,
Whereby from death to life he had been brought;
That dead, his life she was, as she had been
His life's delight while still she lived a queen.
And he fell wondering if his life were gain,
So wrapt as then in loneliness and pain;
Yet therewithal no tears would fill his eyes,
For as a god he was.

Then did he rise
And gat him down unto the Council-place,
And when the people saw his well-loved face
Then cried aloud for joy to see him there.
And earth again to them seemed blest and fair.
And though indeed they did lament in turn,
When of Alcestis' end they came to learn,
Scarce was it more than seeming, or, at least,
The silence in the middle of a feast,
When men have memory of their heroes slain.
So passed the order of the world again,
Victorious Summer crowning lusty Spring,
Rich Autumn faint with wealth of harvesting,
And Winter the earth's sleep; and then again
Spring, Summer, Autumn, and the Winter's pain:
And still and still the same the years went by.

But Time, who slays so many a memory,
Brought hers to light, the short-lived loving Queen;
And her fair soul, as scent of flowers unseen,
Sweetened the turmoil of long centuries.
For soon, indeed, Death laid his hand on these,
The shouters round the throne upon that day.
And for Admetus, he, too, went his way,
Though if he died at all I cannot tell;
But either on the earth he ceased to dwell,
Or else, oft born again, had many a name.
But through all lands of Greece Alcestis' fame
Grew greater, and about her husband's twined

Lived, in the hearts of far-off men enshrined.
See I have told her tale, though I know not
What men are dwelling now on that green spot
Anigh Boebeis, or if Pheræ still,
With name oft changed perchance, adown the hill
Still shows its white walls to the rising sun.
The gods at least remember what is done.

Strange felt the wanderers at his tale, for now
Their old desires it seemed once more to show
Unto their altered hearts, when now the rest,
Most surely coming, of all things seemed best;
Unless, by death perchance they yet might gain
Some space to try such deeds as now in vain
They heard of amidst stories of the past;
Such deeds as they for that wild hope had cast
From out their hands, they sighed to think of it,
And how as deedless men they there must sit.

Yet, with the measured falling of that rhyme
Mingled the lovely sights and glorious time,
Whereby, in spite of hope long past away,
In spite of knowledge growing day by day
Of lives so wasted, in despite of death,
With sweet content that eve they drew their breath,
And scarce their own lives seemed to touch them more
Than that dead Queen's beside Boebéis' shore;
Bitter and sweet so mingled in them both,
Their lives and that old tale, they had been loth,
Perchance, to have them told another way.
So passed the sun from that fair summer day.

June drew unto its end, the hot bright days
Now gat from men as much of blame as praise,
As rainless still they passed, without a cloud,
And growing grey at last, the barley bowed
Before the south-east wind. On such a day
These folk amid the trellised roses lay,
And careless for a little while at least,
Crowned with the mingled blossoms held their feast:
Nor did the garden lack for younger folk,
Who cared no more for burning summer's yoke
Than the sweet breezes of the April-tide;
But through the thick trees wandered far and wide
From sun to shade, and shade to sun again,
Until they deemed the elders would be fain
To hear the tale, and shadows longer grew:
Then round about the grave old men they drew,
Both youths and maidens; and beneath their feet
The grass seemed greener, and the flowers more sweet
Unto the elders, as they stood around.

So through the calm air soon arose the sound
Of one old voice as now a Wanderer spoke.
"O friends, and ye, fair loving gentle folk,
Would I could better tell a tale to-day;
But hark to this, which while our good ship lay
Within the Weser such a while agone,
A Fleming told me, as we sat alone
One Sunday evening in the Rose-garland,
And all the other folk were gone a-land
After their pleasure, like sea-faring men.
Surely I deem it no great wonder then
That I remember everything he said,
Since from that Sunday eve strange fortune led
That keel and me on such a weary way
Well, at the least it serveth you to-day."

THE LADY OF THE LAND

ARGUMENT

A certain man having landed on an island in the Greek Sea found there a beautiful damsel, whom he would fain have delivered from a strange and dreadful doom, but failing herein, he died soon afterwards.

It happened once, some men of Italy
Midst the Greek Islands went a sea-roving,
And much good fortune had they on the sea:
Of many a man they had the ransoming,
And many a chain they gat, and goodly thing;
And midst their voyage to an isle they came,
Whereof my story keepeth not the name.

Now though but little was there left to gain,
Because the richer folk had gone away,
Yet since by this of water they were fain
They came to anchor in a land-locked bay,
Whence in a while some went ashore to play,
Going but lightly armed in twos or threes,
For midst that folk they feared no enemies.

And of these fellows that thus went ashore,
One was there who left all his friends behind;
Who going inland ever more and more,
And being left quite alone, at last did find
A lonely valley sheltered from the wind,
Wherein, amidst an ancient cypress wood,
A long-deserted ruined castle stood.

The wood, once ordered in fair grove and glade,
With gardens overlooked by terraces,
And marble-pavéd pools for pleasure made,
Was tangled now, and choked with fallen trees;
And he who went there, with but little ease
Must stumble by the stream's side, once made meet
For tender women's dainty wandering feet.

The raven's croak, the low wind choked and drear,
The baffled stream, the grey wolf's doleful cry,
Were all the sounds that mariner could hear,
As through the wood he wandered painfully;
But as unto the house he drew anigh,
The pillars of a ruined shrine he saw,
The once fair temple of a fallen law.

No image was there left behind to tell
Before whose face the knees of men had bowed;
An altar of black stone, of old wrought well,
Alone beneath a ruined roof now showed
The goal whereto the folk were wont to crowd,
Seeking for things forgotten long ago,
Praying for heads long ages laid a-low.

Close to the temple was the castle-gate,
Doorless and crumbling; there our fellow turned,
Trembling indeed at what might chance to wait
The prey entrapped, yet with a heart that burned
To know the most of what might there be learned,
And hoping somewhat too, amid his fear,
To light on such things as all men hold dear.

Noble the house was, nor seemed built for war,
But rather like the work of other days,
When men, in better peace than now they are,
Had leisure on the world around to gaze,
And noted well the past times' changing ways;
And fair with sculptured stories it was wrought,
By lapse of time unto dim ruin brought.

Now as he looked about on all these things,
And strove to read the mouldering histories,
Above the door an image with wide wings,
Whose unclad limbs a serpent seemed to seize,
He dimly saw, although the western breeze,
And years of biting frost and washing rain,
Had made the carver's labour well-nigh vain.

But this, though perished sore, and worn away,
He noted well, because it seemed to be,
After the fashion of another day,

Some great man's badge of war, or armoury,
And round it a carved wreath he seemed to see;
But taking note of these things, at the last
The mariner beneath the gateway passed.

And there a lovely cloistered court he found,
A fountain in the midst o'erthrown and dry,
And in the cloister briers twining round
The slender shafts; the wondrous imagery
Outworn by more than many years gone by,
Because the country people, in their fear
Of wizardry, had wrought destruction here;

And piteously these fair things had been maimed;
There stood great Jove, lacking his head of might;
Here was the archer, swift Apollo, lamed;
The shapely limbs of Venus hid from sight
By weeds and shards; Diana's ankles light
Bound with the cable of some coasting ship;
And rusty nails through Helen's maddening lip.

Therefrom unto the chambers did he pass,
And found them fair still, midst of their decay,
Though in them now no sign of man there was,
And everything but stone had passed away
That made them lovely in that vanished day;
Nay, the mere walls themselves would soon be gone
And nought be left but heaps of mouldering stone.

But he, when all the place he had gone o'er.
And with much trouble clomb the broken stair,
And from the topmost turret seen the shore
And his good ship drawn up at anchor there,
Came down again, and found a crypt most fair
Built wonderfully beneath the greatest hall,
And there he saw a door within the wall,

Well-hinged, close shut; nor was there in that place
Another on its hinges, therefore he
Stood there and pondered for a little space,
And thought, "Perchance some marvel I shall see,
For surely here some dweller there must be,
Because this door seems whole, and new, and sound.
While nought but ruin I can see around."

So with that word, moved by a strong desire,
He tried the hasp, that yielded to his hand,
And in a strange place, lit as by a fire
Unseen but near, he presently did stand;
And by an odorous breeze his face was fanned,
As though in some Arabian plain he stood,

Anigh the border of a spice-tree wood.

He moved not for awhile, but looking round,
He wondered much to see the place so fair,
Because, unlike the castle above ground,
No pillager or wrecker had been there;
It seemed that time had passed on otherwhere,
Nor laid a finger on this hidden place,
Rich with the wealth of some forgotten race.

With hangings, fresh as when they left the loom,
The walls were hung a space above the head,
Slim ivory chairs were set about the room,
And in one corner was a dainty bed,
That seemed for some fair queen apparelléd;
And marble was the worst stone of the floor,
That with rich Indian webs was covered o'er.

The wanderer trembled when he saw all this,
Because he deemed by magic it was wrought;
Yet in his heart a longing for some bliss,
Whereof the hard and changing world knows nought,
Arose and urged him on, and dimmed the thought
That there perchance some devil lurked to slay
The heedless wanderer from the light of day.

Over against him was another door
Set in the wall, so, casting fear aside,
With hurried steps he crossed the varied floor,
And there again the silver latch he tried
And with no pain the door he opened wide,
And entering the new chamber cautiously
The glory of great heaps of gold could see.

Upon the floor uncounted medals lay,
Like things of little value; here and there
Stood golden caldrons, that might well outweigh
The biggest midst an emperor's copper-ware,
And golden cups were set on tables fair,
Themselves of gold; and in all hollow things
Were stored great gems, worthy the crowns of kings.

The walls and roof with gold were overlaid,
And precious raiment from the wall hung down;
The fall of kings that treasure might have stayed,
Or gained some longing conqueror great renown,
Or built again some god-destroyed old town;
What wonder, if this plunderer of the sea
Stood gazing at it long and dizzily?

But at the last his troubled eyes and dazed

He lifted from the glory of that gold,
And then the image, that well-nigh erased
Over the castle-gate he did behold,
Above a door well wrought in coloured gold
Again he saw; a naked girl with wings
Enfolded in a serpent's scaly rings.

And even as his eyes were fixed on it
A woman's voice came from the other side,
And through his heart strange hopes began to flit
That in some wondrous land he might abide
Not dying, master of a deathless bride,
So o'er the gold which now he scarce could see
He went, and passed this last door eagerly.

Then in a room he stood wherein there was
A marble bath, whose brimming water yet
Was scarcely still; a vessel of green glass
Half full of odorous ointment was there set
Upon the topmost step that still was wet,
And jewelled shoes and women's dainty gear,
Lay cast upon the varied pavement near.

In one quick glance these things his eyes did see,
But speedily they turned round to behold
Another sight, for throned on ivory
There sat a woman, whose wet tresses rolled
On to the floor in waves of gleaming gold,
Cast back from such a form as, erewhile shown
To one poor shepherd, lighted up Troy town.

Naked she was, the kisses of her feet
Upon the floor a dying path had made
From the full bath unto her ivory seat;
In her right hand, upon her bosom laid,
She held a golden comb, a mirror weighed
Her left hand down, aback her fair head lay
Dreaming awake of some long vanished day.

Her eyes were shut, but she seemed not to sleep,
Her lips were murmuring things unheard and low,
Or sometimes twitched as though she needs must weep
Though from her eyes the tears refused to flow,
And oft with heavenly red her cheek did glow,
As if remembrance of some half-sweet shame
Across the web of many memories came.

There stood the man, scarce daring to draw breath
For fear the lovely sight should fade away;
Forgetting heaven, forgetting life and death,
Trembling for fear lest something he should say

Unwitting, lest some sob should yet betray
His presence there, for to his eager eyes
Already did the tears begin to rise.

But as he gazed she moved, and with a sigh
Bent forward, dropping down her golden head;
"Alas, alas! another day gone by,
Another day and no soul come," she said;
"Another year, and still I am not dead!"
And with that word once more her head she raised,
And on the trembling man with great eyes gazed.

Then he imploring hands to her did reach,
And toward her very slowly 'gan to move
And with wet eyes her pity did beseech,
And seeing her about to speak he strove
From trembling lips to utter words of love;
But with a look she stayed his doubtful feet,
And made sweet music as their eyes did meet.

For now she spoke in gentle voice and clear,
Using the Greek tongue that he knew full well;
"What man art thou, that thus hast wandered here.
And found this lonely chamber where I dwell?
Beware, beware! for I have many a spell;
If greed of power and gold have led thee on,
Not lightly shall this untold wealth be won.

"But if thou com'st here, knowing of my tale,
In hope to bear away my body fair,
Stout must thine heart be, nor shall that avail
If thou a wicked soul in thee dost bear;
So once again I bid thee to beware,
Because no base man things like this may see,
And live thereafter long and happily."

"Lady," he said, "in Florence is my home,
And in my city noble is my name;
Neither on peddling voyage am I come,
But, like my fathers, bent to gather fame;
And though thy face has set my heart a-flame
Yet of thy story nothing do I know,
But here have wandered heedlessly enow.

"But since the sight of thee mine eyes did bless,
What can I be but thine? what wouldst thou have?
From those thy words, I deem from some distress
By deeds of mine thy dear life I might save;
O then, delay not! if one ever gave
His life to any, mine I give to thee;
Come, tell me what the price of love must be?

"Swift death, to be with thee a day and night
And with the earliest dawning to be slain?
Or better, a long year of great delight,
And many years of misery and pain?
Or worse, and this poor hour for all my gain?
A sorry merchant am I on this day,
E'en as thou wiliest so must I obey."

She said, "What brave words! nought divine am I,
But an unhappy and unheard-of maid
Compelled by evil fate and destiny
To live, who long ago should have been laid
Under the earth within the cypress shade.
Hearken awhile, and quickly shalt thou know
What deed I pray thee to accomplish now.

"God grant indeed thy words are not for nought!
Then shalt thou save me, since for many a day
To such a dreadful life I have been brought:
Nor will I spare with all my heart to pay
What man soever takes my grief away;
Ah! I will love thee, if thou lovest me
But well enough my saviour now to be.

"My father lived a many years agone
Lord of this land, master of all cunning,
Who ruddy gold could draw from out grey stone,
And gather wealth from many an uncouth thing,
He made the wilderness rejoice and sing,
And such a leech he was that none could say
Without his word what soul should pass away.

"Unto Diana such a gift he gave,
Goddess above, below, and on the earth,
That I should be her virgin and her slave
From the first hour of my most wretched birth;
Therefore my life had known but little mirth
When I had come unto my twentieth year
And the last time of hallowing drew anear.

"So in her temple had I lived and died
And all would long ago have passed away,
But ere that time came, did strange things betide,
Whereby I am alive unto this day;
Alas, the bitter words that I must say!
Ah! can I bring my wretched tongue to tell
How I was brought unto this fearful hell.

"A queen I was, what gods I knew I loved,
And nothing evil was there in my thought,

And yet by love my wretched heart was moved
Until to utter ruin I was brought!
Alas! thou sayest our gods were vain and nought,
Wait, wait, till thou hast heard this tale of mine.
Then shalt thou think them devilish or divine.

"Hearken! in spite of father and of vow
I loved a man; but for that sin I think
Men had forgiven me, yea, yea, even thou;
But from the gods the full cup must I drink,
And into misery unheard of sink,
Tormented when their own names are forgot,
And men must doubt e'er if they lived or not.

"Glorious my lover was unto my sight,
Most beautiful, of love we grew so fain
That we at last agreed, that on a night
We should be happy, but that he were slain
Or shut in hold, and neither joy nor pain
Should else forbid that hoped-for time to be;
So came the night that made a wretch of me.

"Ah I well do I remember all that night,
When through the window shone the orb of June,
And by the bed flickered the taper's light,
Whereby I trembled, gazing at the moon:
Ah me! the meeting that we had, when soon
Into his strong, well-trusted arms I fell,
And many a sorrow we began to tell.

"Ah me I what parting on that night we had!
I think the story of my great despair
A little while might merry folk make sad;
For, as he swept away my yellow hair
To make my shoulder and my bosom bare,
I raised mine eyes, and shuddering could behold
A shadow cast upon the bed of gold:

"Then suddenly was quenched my hot desire
And he untwined his arms; the moon so pale
A while ago, seemed changed to blood and fire,
And yet my limbs beneath me did not fail,
And neither had I strength to cry or wail,
But stood there helpless, bare, and shivering,
With staring eyes still fixed upon the thing.

"Because the shade that on the bed of gold
The changed and dreadful moon was throwing down
Was of Diana, whom I did behold,
With knotted hair, and shining girt-up gown,
And on the high white brow, a deadly frown

Bent upon us, who stood scarce drawing breath,
Striving to meet the horrible sure death.

"No word at all the dreadful goddess said,
But soon across my feet my lover lay,
And well indeed I knew that he was dead;
And would that I had died on that same day!
For in a while the image turned away,
And without words my doom I understood,
And felt a horror change my human blood.

"And there I fell, and on the floor I lay
By the dead man, till daylight came on me,
And not a word thenceforward could I say
For three years, till of grief and misery,
The lingering pest, the cruel enemy,
My father and his folk were dead and gone,
And in this castle I was left alone:

"And then the doom foreseen upon me fell,
For Queen Diana did my body change
Into a fork-tongued dragon flesh and fell,
And through the island nightly do I range,
Or in the green sea mate with monsters strange,
When in the middle of the moonlit night
The sleepy mariner I do affright.

"But all day long upon this gold I lie
Within this place, where never mason's hand
Smote trowel on the marble noisily;
Drowsy I lie, no folk at my command,
Who once was called the Lady of the Land;
Who might have bought a kingdom with a kiss,
Yea, half the world with such a sight as this."

And therewithal, with rosy fingers light,
Backward her heavy-hanging hair she threw,
To give her naked beauty more to sight;
But when, forgetting all the things he knew,
Maddened with love unto the prize he drew,
She cried, "Nay, wait! for wherefore wilt thou die,
Why should we not be happy, thou and I?

"Wilt thou not save me? once in every year
This rightful form of mine that thou dost see
By favour of the goddess have I here
From sunrise unto sunset given me,
That some brave man may end my misery.
And thou, art thou not brave? can thy heart fail,
Whose eyes e'en now are weeping at my tale?

"Then listen! when this day is overpast,
A fearful monster shall I be again,
And thou mayst be my saviour at the last,
Unless, once more, thy words are nought and vain;
If thou of love and sovereignty art fain,
Come thou next morn, and when thou seest here
A hideous dragon, have thereof no fear,

"But take the loathsome head up in thine hands,
And kiss it, and be master presently
Of twice the wealth that is in all the lands,
From Cathay to the head of Italy;
And master also, if it pleaseth thee,
Of all thou praisest as so fresh and bright,
Of what thou callest crown of all delight.

"Ah! with what joy then shall I see again
The sunlight on the green grass and the trees,
And hear the clatter of the summer rain,
And see the joyous folk beyond the seas.
Ah, me! to hold my child upon my knees,
After the weeping of unkindly tears,
And all the wrongs of these four hundred years.

"Go now, go quick! leave this grey heap of stone;
And from thy glad heart think upon thy way,
How I shall love thee, yea, love thee alone,
That bringest me from dark death unto day;
For this shall be thy wages and thy pay;
Unheard-of wealth, unheard-of love is near,
If thou hast heart a little dread to bear."

Therewith she turned to go; but he cried out,
"Ah! wilt thou leave me then without one kiss,
To slay the very seeds of fear and doubt,
That glad to-morrow may bring certain bliss?
Hast thou forgotten how love lives by this,
The memory of some hopeful close embrace,
Low whispered words within some lonely place?"

But she, when his bright glittering eyes she saw,
And burning cheeks, cried out, "Alas, alas!
Must I be quite undone, and wilt thou draw
A worse fate on me than the first one was?
O haste thee from this fatal place to pass!
Yet, ere thou goest, take this, lest thou shouldst deem
Thou hast been fooled by some strange midday dream."

So saying, blushing like a new-kissed maid,
From off her neck a little gem she drew,
That, 'twixt those snowy rose-tinged hillocks laid,

The secrets of her glorious beauty knew;
And ere he well perceived what she would do,
She touched his hand, the gem within it lay,
And, turning, from his sight she fled away.

Then at the doorway where her rosy heel
Had glanced and vanished, he awhile did stare,
And still upon his hand he seemed to feel
The varying kisses of her fingers fair;
Then turned he toward the dreary crypt and bare,
And dizzily throughout the castle passed,
Till by the ruined fane he stood at last.

Then weighing still the gem within his hand,
He stumbled backward through the cypress wood,
Thinking the while of some strange lovely land,
Where all his life should be most fair and good;
Till on the valley's wall of hills he stood,
And slowly thence passed down unto the bay
Red with the death of that bewildering day.

The next day came, and he, who all the night
Had ceaselessly been turning in his bed,
Arose and clad himself in armour bright,
And many a danger he rememberéd;
Storming of towns, lone sieges full of dread,
That with renown his heart had borne him through,
And this thing seemed a little thing to do.

So on he went, and on the way he thought
Of all the glorious things of yesterday,
Nought of the price whereat they must be bought,
But ever to himself did softly say,
"No roaming now, my wars are passed away,
No long dull days devoid of happiness,
When such a love my yearning heart shall bless."

Thus to the castle did he come at last,
But when unto the gateway he drew near,
And underneath its ruined archway passed
Into the court, a strange noise did he hear,
And through his heart there shot a pang of fear,
Trembling, he gat his sword into his hand,
And midmost of the cloisters took his stand.

But for a while that unknown noise increased
A rattling, that with strident roars did blend,
And whining moans; but suddenly it ceased,
A fearful thing stood at the cloister's end,
And eyed him for a while, then 'gan to wend
Adown the cloisters, and began again

That rattling, and the moan like fiends in pain.

And as it came on towards him, with its teeth
The body of a slain goat did it tear,
The blood whereof in its hot jaws did seethe,
And on its tongue he saw the smoking hair;
Then his heart sank, and standing trembling there,
Throughout his mind wild thoughts and fearful ran,
"Some fiend she was," he said, "the bane of man."

Yet he abode her still, although his blood
Curdled within him: the thing dropped the goat,
And creeping on, came close to where he stood,
And raised its head to him, and wrinkled throat,
Then he cried out and wildly at her smote,
Shutting his eyes, and turned and from the place
Ran swiftly, with a white and ghastly face.

But little things rough stones and tree-trunks seemed,
And if he fell, he rose and ran on still;
No more he felt his hurts than if he dreamed,
He made no stay for valley or steep hill,
Heedless he dashed through many a foaming rill,
Until he came unto the ship at last
And with no word into the deep hold passed.

Meanwhile the dragon, seeing him clean gone.
Followed him not, but crying horribly, ·
Caught up within her jaws a block of stone
And ground it into powder, then turned she,
With cries that folk could hear far out at sea,
And reached the treasure set apart of old,
To brood above the hidden heaps of gold.

Yet was she seen again on many a day
By some half-waking mariner, or herd,
Playing amid the ripples of the bay,
Or on the hills making all things afeard,
Or in the wood, that did that castle gird,
But never any man again durst go
To seek her woman's form, and end her woe.

As for the man, who knows what things he bore?
What mournful faces peopled the sad night,
What wailings vexed him with reproaches sore,
What images of that nigh-gained delight!
What dreamed caresses from soft hands and white,
Turning to horrors ere they reached the best,
What struggles vain, what shame, what huge unrest?

No man he knew, three days he lay and raved,

And cried for death, until a lethargy
Fell on him, and his fellows thought him saved;
But on the third night he awoke to die;
And at Byzantium doth his body lie
Between two blossoming pomegranate trees,
Within the churchyard of the Genoese.

A moment's silence as his tale had end,
And then the wind of that June night did blend
Their varied voices, as of that and this
They fell to talk: of those fair islands' bliss
They knew in other days, of hope they had
To live there long an easy life and glad,
With nought to vex them; and the younger men
Began to nourish strange dreams even then
Of sailing east, as these had once sailed west;
Because the story of that luckless quest
With hope, not fear, had filled their joyous hearts
And made them dream of new and noble parts
That they might act; of raising up the name
Their fathers bore, and winning boundless fame.
These too with little patience seemed to hear,
That story end with shame and grief and fear;
A little thing the man had had to do,
They said, if longing burned within him so.
But at their words the older men must bow
Their heads, and, smiling, somewhat thoughtful grow,
Remembering well how fear in days gone by
Had dealt with them, and poisoned wretchedly
Good days, good deeds, and longings for all good:
Yet on the evil times they would not brood,
But sighing, strove to raise the weight of years,
And no more memory of their hopes and fears
They nourished, but such gentle thoughts as fed
The pensiveness which that sweet season bred.

JULY

Fair was the morn to-day, the blossom's scent
Floated across the fresh grass, and the bees
With low vexed song from rose to lily went,
A gentle wind was in the heavy trees,
And thine eyes shone with joyous memories;
Fair was the early morn, and fair wert thou,
And I was happy. Ah, be happy now!

Peace and content without us, love within
That hour there was, now thunder and wild rain,
Have wrapped the cowering world, and foolish sin,

And nameless pride, have made us wise in vain;
Ah, love! although the morn shall come again,
And on new rose-buds the new sun shall smile,
Can we regain what we have lost meanwhile?

E'en now the west grows clear of storm and threat,
But midst the lightning did the fair sun die
Ah, he shall rise again for ages yet,
He cannot waste his life, but thou and I
Who knows if next morn this felicity
My lips may feel, or if thou still shalt live
This seal of love renewed once more to give?

Within a lovely valley, watered well
With flowery streams, the July feast befell,
And there within the Chief-priest's fair abode
They cast aside their trouble's heavy load,
Scarce made aweary by the sultry day.
The earth no longer laboured; shaded lay
The sweet-breathed kine, across the sunny vale,
From hill to hill the wandering rook did sail,
Lazily croaking, midst his dreams of spring,
Nor more awake the pink-foot dove did cling
Unto the beech-bough, murmuring now and then;
All rested but the restless sons of men
And the great sun that wrought this happiness,
And all the vale with fruitful hopes did bless.
So in a marble chamber bright with flowers,
The old men feasted through the fresher hours,
And at the hottest time of all the day
When now the sun was on his downward way,
Sat listening to a tale an elder told,
New to his fathers while they yet did hold
The cities of some far-off Grecian isle,
Though in the heavens the cloud of force and guile
Was gathering dark that sent them o'er the sea
To win new lands for their posterity.

THE SON OF CROESUS

ARGUMENT

Croesus, King of Lydia, dreamed that he saw his son slain by an iron weapon, and though by every means he strove to avert this doom from him, yet thus it happened, for his son was slain by the hand of the man who seemed least of all likely to do the deed.

Of Croesus tells my tale, a king of old
In Lydia, ere the Mede fell on the land,
A man made mighty by great heaps of gold,

Feared for the myriads strong of heart and hand
That 'neath his banners wrought out his command,
And though his latter ending happed on ill,
Yet first of every joy he had his fill.

Two sons he had, and one was dumb from birth;
The other one, that Atys had to name,
Grew up a fair youth, and of might and worth,
And well it seemed the race wherefrom he came
From him should never get reproach or shame:
But yet no stroke he struck before his death,
In no war-shout he spent his latest breath.

Now Croesus, lying on his bed anight
Dreamed that he saw this dear son laid a-low,
And folk lamenting he was slain outright,
And that some iron thing had dealt the blow;
By whose hand guided he could nowise know,
Or if in peace by traitors it were done,
Or in some open war not yet begun.

Three times one night this vision broke his sleep,
So that at last he rose up from his bed,
That he might ponder how he best might keep
The threatened danger from so dear a head;
And, since he now was old enough to wed,
The King sent men to search the lands around,
Until some matchless maiden should be found;

That in her arms this Atys might forget
The praise of men, and fame of history,
Whereby full many a field has been made wet
With blood of men, and many a deep green sea
Been reddened therewithal, and yet shall be;
That her sweet voice might drown the people's praise,
Her eyes make bright the uneventful days.

So when at last a wonder they had brought,
From some sweet land down by the ocean's rim.
Than whom no fairer could by man be thought,
And ancient dames, scanning her limb by limb,
Had said that she was fair enough for him,
To her was Atys married with much show,
And looked to dwell with her in bliss enow.

And in meantime afield he never went,
Either to hunting or the frontier war,
No dart was cast, nor any engine bent
Anigh him, and the Lydian men afar
Must rein their steeds, and the bright blossoms mar
If they have any lust of tourney now,

And in far meadows must they bend the bow.

And also through the palace everywhere
The swords and spears were taken from the wall
That long with honour had been hanging there,
And from the golden pillars of the hall;
Lest by mischance some sacred blade should fall,
And in its falling bring revenge at last
For many a fatal battle overpast.

And every day King Croesus wrought with care
To save his dear son from that threatened end,
And many a beast he offered up with prayer
Unto the gods, and much of wealth did spend,
That they so prayed might yet perchance defend
That life, until at least that he were dead,
With earth laid heavy on his unseeing head.

But in the midst even of the wedding feast
There came a man, who by the golden hall
Sat down upon the steps, and man or beast
He heeded not, but there against the wall
He leaned his head, speaking no word at all,
Till, with his son and son's wife, came the King,
And then unto his gown the man did cling.

"What man art thou?" the King said to him then,
"That in such guise thou prayest on thy knee;
Hast thou some fell foe here among my men?
Or hast thou done an ill deed unto me?
Or has thy wife been carried over sea?
Or hast thou on this day great need of gold?
Or say, why else thou now art grown so bold."

"O King," he said, "I ask no gold to-day,
And though indeed thy greatness drew me here,
No wrong have I that thou couldst wipe away;
And nought of mine the pirate folk did bear
Across the sea; none of thy folk I fear:
But all the gods are now mine enemies,
Therefore I kneel before thee on my knees.

"For as with mine own brother on a day
Within the running place at home I played,
Unwittingly I smote him such-a-way
That dead upon the green grass he was laid;
Half-dead myself I fled away dismayed,
Wherefore I pray thee help me in my need,
And purify my soul of this sad deed.

"If of my name and country thou wouldst know,

In Phrygia yet my father is a king,
Gordius, the son of Midas, rich enow
In corn and cattle, golden cup and ring;
And mine own name before I did this thing
Was called Adrastus, whom, in street and hall,
The slayer of his brother men now call."

"Friend," said the King, "have thou no fear of me;
For though, indeed, I am right happy now,
Yet well I know this may not always be,
And I may chance some day to kneel full low,
And to some happy man mine head to bow
With prayers to do a greater thing than this,
Dwell thou with us, and win again thy bliss.

"For in this city men in sport and play
Forget the trouble that the gods have sent;
Who therewithal send wine, and many a may
As fair as she for whom the Trojan went,
And many a dear delight besides have lent,
Which, whoso is well loved of them shall keep
Till in forgetful death he falls asleep.

"Therefore to-morrow shall those rites be done
That kindred blood demands that thou hast shed,
That if the mouth of thine own mother's son
Did hap to curse thee ere he was quite dead,
The curse may lie the lighter on thine head,
Because the flower-crowned head of many a beast
Has fallen voiceless in our glorious feast."

Then did Adrastus rise and thank the King,
And the next day when yet low was the sun,
The sacrifice and every other thing
That unto these dread rites belonged, was done;
And there Adrastus dwelt, hated of none,
And loved of many, and the King loved him,
For brave and wise he was and strong of limb.

But chiefly amongst all did Atys love
The luckless stranger, whose fair tales of war
The Lydian's heart abundantly did move,
And much they talked of wandering out afar
Some day, to lands where many marvels are,
With still the Phrygian through all things to be
The leader unto all felicity.

Now at this time folk came unto the King
Who on a forest's borders dwelling were,
Wherein there roamed full many a dangerous thing,
As wolf and wild bull, lion and brown bear;

But chiefly in that forest was the lair
Of a great boar that no man could withstand.
And many a woe he wrought upon the land.

Since long ago that men in Calydon
Held chase, no beast like him had once been seen
He ruined vineyards lying in the sun,
After his harvesting the men must glean
What he had left; right glad they had not been
Among the tall stalks of the ripening wheat,
The fell destroyer's fatal tusks to meet.

For often would the lonely man entrapped
In vain from his dire fury strive to hide
In some thick hedge, and other whiles it happed
Some careless stranger by his place would ride,
And the tusks smote his fallen horse's side,
And what help then to such a wretch could come
With sword he could not draw, and far from home?

Or else girls, sent their water-jars to fill,
Would come back pale, too terrified to cry,
Because they had but seen him from the hill;
Or else again with side rent wretchedly,
Some hapless damsel midst the brake would lie.
Shortly to say, there neither man nor maid
Was safe afield whether they wrought or played.

Therefore were come these dwellers by the wood
To pray the King brave men to them to send,
That they might live; and if he deemed it good,
That Atys with the other knights should wend,
They thought their grief the easier should have end;
For both by gods and men they knew him loved,
And easily by hope of glory moved.

"O Sire," they said, "thou know'st how Hercules
Was not content to wait till folk asked aid,
But sought the pests among their guarded trees;
Thou know'st what name the Theban Cadmus made,
And how the bull of Marathon was laid
Dead on the fallows of the Athenian land,
And how folk worshipped Atalanta's hand.

"Fair would thy son's name look upon the roll
Wherein such noble deeds as this are told;
And great delight shall surely fill thy soul,
Thinking upon his deeds when thou art old,
And thy brave heart is waxen faint and cold:
Dost thou not know, O King, how men will strive
That they, when dead, still in their sons may live?"

He shuddered as they spoke, because he thought,
Most certainly a winning tale is this
To draw him from the net where he is caught,
For hearts of men grow weary of all bliss;
Nor is he one to be content with his,
If he should hear the trumpet-blast of fame
And far-off people calling on his name.

"Good friends," he said, "go, get ye back again.
And doubt not I will send you men to slay
This pest ye fear: yet shall your prayer be vain
If ye with any other speak to-day;
And for my son, with me he needs must stay,
For mighty cares oppress the Lydian land.
Fear not, for ye shall have a noble band."

And with that promise must they be content,
And so departed, having feasted well.
And yet some god or other ere they went,
If they were silent, this their tale must tell
To more than one man; therefore it befell,
That at the last Prince Atys knew the thing,
And came with angry eyes unto the King.

"Father," he said, "since when am I grown vile
Since when am I grown helpless of my hands?
Or else what folk, with words enwrought with guile
Thine ears have poisoned; that when far-off lands
My fame might fill, by thy most strange commands
I needs must stay within this slothful home,
Whereto would God that I had never come?

"What! wilt thou take mine honour quite away
Wouldst thou, that, as with her I just have wed
I sit among thy folk at end of day,
She should be ever turning round her head
To watch some man for war apparelled
Because he wears a sword that he may use,
Which grace to me thou ever wilt refuse?

"Or dost thou think, when thou hast run thy race
And thou art gone, and in thy stead I reign,
The people will do honour to my place,
Or that the lords leal men will still remain,
If yet my father's sword be sharp in vain?
If on the wall his armour still hang up,
While for a spear I hold a drinking-cup?"

"O Son!" quoth Croesus, "well I know thee brave
And worthy of high deeds of chivalry;

Therefore the more thy dear life would I save,
Which now is threatened by the gods on high;
Three times one night I dreamed I saw thee die,
Slain by some deadly iron-pointed thing,
While weeping lords stood round thee in a ring."

Then loud laughed Atys, and he said again,
"Father, and did this ugly dream tell thee
What day it was on which I should be slain?
As may the gods grant I may one day be,
And not from sickness die right wretchedly,
Groaning with pain, my lords about my bed,
Wishing to God that I were fairly dead;

"But slain in battle, as the Lydian kings
Have died ere now, in some great victory,
While all about the Lydian shouting rings
Death to the beaten foemen as they fly.
What death but this, O father! should I die?
But if my life by iron shall be done,
What steel to-day shall glitter in the sun?

"Yea, father, if to thee it seemeth good
To keep me from the bright steel-bearing throng,
Let me be brave at least within the wood;
For surely, if thy dream be true, no wrong
Can hap to me from this beast's tushes strong:
Unless perchance the beast is grown so wise,
He haunts the forest clad in Lydian guise."

Then Croesus said: "O Son, I love thee so,
That thou shalt do thy will upon this tide:
But since unto this hunting thou must go,
A trusty friend along with thee shall ride,
Who not for anything shall leave thy side.
I think, indeed, he loves thee well enow
To thrust his heart 'twixt thee and any blow.

"Go then, O Son, and if by some short span
Thy life be measured, how shall it harm thee,
If while life last thou art a happy man?
And thou art happy; only unto me
Is trembling left, and infelicity:
The trembling of the man who loves on earth,
But unto thee is hope and present mirth.

"Nay, be thou not ashamed, for on this day
I fear not much: thou read'st my dream aright,
No teeth or claws shall take thy life away.
And it may chance, ere thy last glorious fight,
I shall be blinded by the endless night;

And brave Adrastus on this day shall be
Thy safeguard, and shall give good heart to me.

"Go then, and send him hither, and depart;
And as the heroes did so mayst thou do,
Winning such fame as well may please thine heart."
With that word from the King did Atys go,
Who, left behind, sighed, saying, "May it be so,
Even as I hope; and yet I would to God
These men upon my threshold ne'er had trod."

So when Adrastus to the King was come
He said unto him, "O my Phrygian friend,
We in this land have given thee a home,
And 'gainst all foes your life will we defend:
Wherefore for us that life thou shouldest spend,
If any day there should be need therefor;
And now a trusty friend I need right sore.

"Doubtless ere now thou hast heard many say
There is a doom that threatens my son's life;
Therefore this place is stript of arms to-day,
And therefore still bides Atys with his wife,
And tempts not any god by raising strife;
Yet none the less by no desire of his,
To whom would war be most abundant bliss.

"And since to-day some glory he may gain
Against a monstrous bestial enemy
And that the meaning of my dream is plain;
That saith that he by steel alone shall die,
His burning wish I may not well deny,
Therefore afield to-morrow doth he wend
And herein mayst thou show thyself my friend

"For thou as captain of his band shalt ride,
And keep a watchful eye of everything,
Nor leave him whatsoever may betide:
Lo, thou art brave, the son of a great king,
And with thy praises doth this city ring,
Why should I tell thee what a name those gain,
Who dying for their friends, die not in vain?"

Then said Adrastus, "Now were I grown base
Beyond all words, if I should spare for aught
In guarding him, so sit with smiling face,
And of this matter take no further thought,
Because with my life shall his life be bought,
If ill should hap; and no ill fate it were,
If I should die for what I hold so dear."

Then went Adrastus, and next morn all things,
That 'longed unto the hunting were well dight,
And forth they went clad as the sons of kings,
Fair was the morn, as through the sunshine bright
They rode, the Prince half wild with great delight,
The Phrygian smiling on him soberly,
And ever looking round with watchful eye.

So through the city all the rout rode fast,
With many a great black-muzzled yellow hound;
And then the teeming country-side they passed,
Until they came to sour and rugged ground,
And there rode up a little heathy mound,
That overlooked the scrubby woods and low,
That of the beast's lair somewhat they might know.

And there a good man of the country-side
Showed them the places where he mostly lay;
And they, descending, through the wood did ride,
And followed on his tracks for half the day.
And at the last they brought him well to bay,
Within an oozy space amidst the wood,
About the which a ring of alders stood.

So when the hounds' changed voices clear they heard
With hearts aflame on towards him straight they drew
Atys the first of all, of nought afeard,
Except that folk should say some other slew
The beast; and lustily his horn he blew,
Going afoot; then, mighty spear in hand,
Adrastus headed all the following band.

Now when they came unto the plot of ground
Where stood the boar, hounds dead about him lay
Or sprawled about, bleeding from many a wound,
But still the others held him well at bay,
Nor had he been bestead thus ere that day.
But yet, seeing Atys, straight he rushed at him,
Speckled with foam, bleeding in flank and limb.

Then Atys stood and cast his well-steeled spear
With a great shout, and straight and well it flew;
For now the broad blade cutting through the ear,
A stream of blood from out the shoulder drew.
And therewithal another, no less true,
Adrastus cast, whereby the boar had died:
But Atys drew the bright sword from his side,

And to the tottering beast he drew anigh:
But as the sun's rays ran adown the blade
Adrastus threw a javelin hastily,

For of the mighty beast was he afraid,
Lest by his wounds he should not yet be stayed,
But with a last rush cast his life away,
And dying there, the son of Croesus slay.

But even as the feathered dart he hurled,
His strained, despairing eyes, beheld the end,
And changed seemed all the fashion of the world,
And past and future into one did blend,
As he beheld the fixed eyes of his friend,
That no reproach had in them, and no fear,
For Death had seized him ere he thought him near.

Adrastus shrieked, and running up he caught
The falling man, and from his bleeding side
Drew out the dart, and, seeing that death had brought
Deliverance to him, he thereby had died;
But ere his hand the luckless steel could guide,
And he the refuge of poor souls could win,
The horror-stricken huntsmen had rushed in.

And these, with blows and cries he heeded nought
His unresisting hands made haste to bind;
Then of the alder-boughs a bier they wrought,
And laid the corpse thereon, and 'gan to wind
Homeward amidst the tangled wood and blind,
And going slowly, at the eventide,
Some leagues from Sardis did that day abide.

Onward next morn the slaughtered man they bore,
With him that slew him, and at end of day
They reached the city, and with mourning sore
Toward the King's palace did they take their way.
He in an open western chamber lay
Feasting, though inwardly his heart did burn
Until that Atys should to him return.

And when those wails first smote upon his ear
He set the wine-cup down, and to his feet
He rose, and bitter all-consuming fear
Swallowed his joy, and nigh he went to meet
That which was coming through the weeping street;
But in the end he thought it good to wait,
And stood there doubting all the ills of fate.

But when at last up to that royal place
Folk brought the thing he once had held so dear
Still stood the King, staring with ghastly face
As they brought forth Adrastus and the bier,
But spoke at last, slowly without a tear,
"O Phrygian man, that I did purify,

Is it through thee that Atys came to die?"

"O King," Adrastus said, "take now my life,
With whatso torment seemeth good to thee,
As my word went, for I would end this strife,
And underneath the earth lie quietly;
Nor is it my will here alive to be:
For as my brother, so Prince Atys died,
And this unlucky hand some god did guide."

Then as a man constrained, the tale he told
From end to end, nor spared himself one whit:
And as he spoke, the wood did still behold,
The trodden grass, and Atys dead on it;
And many a change o'er the King's face did flit
Of kingly rage, and hatred and despair,
As on the slayer's face he still did stare.

At last he said, "Thy death avails me nought.
The gods themselves have done this bitter deed,
That I was all too happy was their thought,
Therefore thy heart is dead and mine doth bleed,
And I am helpless as a trodden weed:
Thou art but as the handle of the spear,
The caster sits far off from any fear.

"Yet, if thy hurt they meant, I can do this,
Loose him and let him go in peace from me
I will not slay the slayer of all my bliss;
Yet go, poor man, for when thy face I see
I curse the gods for their felicity.
Surely some other slayer they would have found,
If thou hadst long ago been under ground.

"Alas, Adrastus! in my inmost heart
I knew the gods would one day do this thing,
But deemed indeed that it would be thy part
To comfort me amidst my sorrowing;
Make haste to go, for I am still a King!
Madness may take me, I have many hands
Who will not spare to do my worst commands."

With that Adrastus' bonds were done away,
And forthwith to the city gates he ran,
And on the road where they had been that day
Rushed through the gathering night; and some lone man
Beheld next day his visage wild and wan,
Peering from out a thicket of the wood
Where he had spilt that well-belovéd blood.

And now the day of burial pomp must be,

And to those rites all lords of Lydia came
About the King, and that day, they and he
Cast royal gifts of rich things on the flame;
But while they stood and wept, and called by name
Upon the dead, amidst them came a man
With raiment rent, and haggard face and wan:

Who when the marshals would have thrust him out
And men looked strange on him, began to say,
"Surely the world is changed since ye have doubt
Of who I am; nay, turn me not away,
For ye have called me princely ere to-day
Adrastus, son of Gordius, a great king,
Where unto Pallas Phrygian maidens sing.

"O Lydians, many a rich thing have ye cast
Into this flame, but I myself will give
A greater gift, since now I see at last
The gods are wearied for that still I live,
And with their will, why should I longer strive?
Atys, O Atys, thus I give to thee
A life that lived for thy felicity."

And therewith from his side a knife he drew,
And, crying out, upon the pile he leapt,
And with one mighty stroke himself he slew.
So there these princes both together slept,
And their light ashes, gathered up, were kept
Within a golden vessel wrought all o'er
With histories of this hunting of the boar.

A gentle wind had risen midst his tale,
That bore the sweet scents of the fertile vale
In at the open windows; and these men
The burden of their years scarce noted then,
Soothed by the sweet luxurious summer time,
And by the cadence of that ancient rhyme,
Spite of its saddening import; nay, indeed,
Of some such thoughts the Wanderers had need
As that tale gave them. Yea, a man shall be
A wonder for his glorious chivalry,
First in all wisdom, of a prudent mind,
Yet none the less him too his fate shall find
Unfenced by these, a man 'mongst other men.
Yea, and will Fortune pick out, now and then,
The noblest for the anvil of her blows;
Great names are few, and yet, indeed, who knows
What greater souls have fallen 'neath the stroke
Of careless fate? Purblind are most of folk,
The happy are the masters of the earth
Which ever give small heed to hapless worth;

So goes the world, and this we needs must bear
Like eld and death: yet there were some men there
Who drank in silence to the memory
Of those who failed on earth great men to be,
Though better than the men who won the crown.
But when the sun was fairly going down
They left the house, and, following up the stream,
In the low sun saw the kingfisher gleam
'Twixt bank and alder, and the grebe steal out
From the high sedge, and, in his restless doubt,
Dive down, and rise to see what men were there:
They saw the swallow chase high up in air
The circling gnats; the shaded dusky pool
Broke by the splashing chub; the ripple cool,
Rising and falling, of some distant weir
They heard, till it oppressed the listening ear,
As twilight grew: so back they turned again
Glad of their rest, and pleasure after pain.

Within the gardens once again they met,
That now the roses did well-nigh forget,
For hot July was drawing to an end,
And August came the fainting year to mend
With fruit and grain; so 'neath the trellises,
Nigh blossomless, did they lie well at ease,
And watched the poppies burn across the grass,
And o'er the bindweed's bells the brown bee pass
Still murmuring of his gains: windless and bright
The morn had been, to help their dear delight;
But heavy clouds ere noon grew round the sun,
And, halfway to the zenith, wild and dun
The sky grew, and the thunder growled afar;
But, ere the steely clouds began their war,
A change there came, and, as by some great hand,
The clouds that hung in threatening o'er the land
Were drawn away; then a light wind arose
That shook the light stems of that flowery close,
And made men sigh for pleasure; therewithal
Did mirth upon the feasting elders fall,
And they no longer watched the lowering sky,
But called aloud for some new history.
Then spoke the Suabian, "Sirs, this tale is told
Among our searchers for fine stones and gold,
And though I tell it wrong be good to me;
For I the written book did never see,
Made by some Fleming, as I think, wherein
Is told this tale of wilfulness and sin."

THE WATCHING OF THE FALCON

The case of this falcon was such, that whoso watched it without sleeping for seven days and seven nights, had his first wish granted him by a fay lady, that appeared to him thereon; and some wished one thing, and some another. But a certain king, who watched the falcon daily, would wish for nought but the love of that fay; which wish being accomplished, was afterwards his ruin.

Across the sea a land there is,
Where, if fate will, may men have bliss,
For it is fair as any land:
There hath the reaper a full hand,
While in the orchard hangs aloft
The purple fig, a-growing soft;
And fair the trellised vine-bunches
Are swung across the high elm-trees;
And in the rivers great fish play,
While over them pass day by day
The laden barges to their place.
There maids are straight, and fair of face,
And men are stout for husbandry,
And all is well as it can be
Upon this earth where all has end.
For on them God is pleased to send
The gift of Death down from above.
That envy, hatred, and hot love,
Knowledge with hunger by his side,
And avarice and deadly pride,
There may have end like everything
Both to the shepherd and the king:
Lest this green earth become but hell
If folk for ever there should dwell.
Full little most men think of this,
But half in woe and half in bliss
They pass their lives, and die at last
Unwilling, though their lot be cast
In wretched places of the earth,
Where men have little joy from birth
Until they die; in no such case
Were those who tilled this pleasant place.
There soothly men were loth to die,
Though sometimes in his misery
A man would say "Would I were dead!"
Alas! full little likelihead
That he should live for ever there.
So folk within that country fair
Lived on, nor from their memories drave
The thought of what they could not have.
And without need tormented still
Each other with some bitter ill;
Yea, and themselves too, growing grey

With dread of some long-lingering day,
That never came ere they were dead
With green sods growing on the head;
Nowise content with what they had,
But falling still from good to bad
While hard they sought the hopeless best
And seldom happy or at rest
Until at last with lessening blood
One foot within the grave they stood.

Now so it chanced that in this land
There did a certain castle stand,
Set all alone deep in the hills,
Amid the sound of falling rills
Within a valley of sweet grass,
To which there went one narrow pass
Through the dark hills, but seldom trod.
Rarely did horse-hoof press the sod
About the quiet weedy moat,
Where unscared did the great fish float;
Because men dreaded there to see
The uncouth things of faërie;
Nathless by some few fathers old
These tales about the place were told
That neither squire nor seneschal
Or varlet came in bower or hall,
Yet all things were in order due,
Hangings of gold and red and blue,
And tables with fair service set;
Cups that had paid the Cæsar's debt
Could he have laid his hands on them;
Dorsars, with pearls in every hem,
And fair embroidered gold-wrought things,
Fit for a company of kings;
And in the chambers dainty beds,
With pillows dight for fair young heads;
And horses in the stables were,
And in the cellars wine full clear
And strong, and casks of ale and mead;
Yea, all things a great lord could need.
For whom these things were ready there
None knew; but if one chanced to fare
Into that place at Easter-tide,
There would he find a falcon tied
Unto a pillar of the Hall;
And such a fate to him would fall,
That if unto the seventh night,
He watched the bird from dark to light,
And light to dark unceasingly,
On the last evening he should see
A lady beautiful past words;

Then, were he come of clowns or lords,
Son of a swineherd or a king,
There must she grant him anything
Perforce, that he might dare to ask,
And do his very hardest task
But if he slumbered, ne'er again
The wretch would wake for he was slain
Helpless, by hands he could not see,
And torn and mangled wretchedly.

Now said these elders. Ere this tide
Full many folk this thing have tried,
But few have got much good thereby;
For first, a many came to die
By slumbering ere their watch was done;
Or else they saw that lovely one,
And mazed, they knew not what to say;
Or asked some toy for all their pay,
That easily they might have won,
Nor staked their lives and souls thereon;
Or asking, asked for some great thing
That was their bane; as to be king
One asked, and died the morrow morn
That he was crowned, of all forlorn.
Yet thither came a certain man,
Who from being poor great riches wan
Past telling, whose grandsons now are
Great lords thereby in peace and war.
And in their coat-of-arms they bear,
Upon a field of azure fair,
A castle and a falcon, set
Below a chief of golden fret.
And in our day a certain knight
Prayed to be worsted in no fight,
And so it happed to him: yet he
Died none the less most wretchedly.
And all his prowess was in vain,
For by a losel was he slain,
As on the highway side he slept
One summer night, of no man kept.

Such tales as these the fathers old
About that lonely castle told;
And in their day the King must try
Himself to prove that mystery,
Although, unless the fay could give
For ever on the earth to live,
Nought could he ask that he had not:
For boundless riches had he got,
Fair children, and a faithful wife;
And happily had passed his life,

And all fulfilled of victory,
Yet was he fain this thing to see.
So towards the mountains he set out
One noontide, with a gallant rout
Of knights and lords, and as the day
Began to fail came to the way
Where he must enter all alone,
Between the dreary walls of stone.
Thereon to that fair company
He bade farewell, who wistfully
Looked backward oft as home they rode,
But in the entry he abode
Of that rough unknown narrowing pass,
Where twilight at the high noon was.
Then onward he began to ride:
Smooth rose the rocks on every side,
And seemed as they were cut by man;
Adown them ever water ran,
But they of living things were bare,
Yea, not a blade of grass grew there;
And underfoot rough was the way,
For scattered all about there lay
Great jagged pieces of black stone.
Throughout the pass the wind did moan,
With such wild noises, that the King
Could almost think he heard something
Spoken of men; as one might hear
The voices of folk standing near
One's chamber wall: yet saw he nought
Except those high walls strangely wrought,
And overhead the strip of sky.
So, going onward painfully,
He met therein no evil thing,
But came about the sun-setting
Unto the opening of the pass,
And thence beheld a vale of grass
Bright with the yellow daffodil;
And all the vale the sun did fill
With his last glory. Midmost there
Rose up a stronghold, built four-square,
Upon a flowery grassy mound,
That moat and high wall ran around.
Thereby he saw a walled pleasance,
With walks and sward fit for the dance
Of Arthur's court in its best time,
That seemed to feel some magic clime;
For though through all the vale outside
Things were as in the April-tide,
And daffodils and cowslips grew
And hidden the March violets blew,
Within the bounds of that sweet close

Was trellised the bewildering rose;
There was the lily over-sweet,
And starry pinks for garlands meet;
And apricots hung on the wall
And midst the flowers did peaches fall,
And nought had blemish there or spot.
For in that place decay was not.

Silent awhile the King abode
Beholding all, then on he rode
And to the castle-gate drew nigh,
Till fell the drawbridge silently,
And when across it he did ride
He found the great gates open wide,
And entered there, but as he passed
The gates were shut behind him fast,
But not before that he could see
The drawbridge rise up silently.
Then round he gazed oppressed with awe,
And there no living thing he saw
Except the sparrows in the eaves,
As restless as light autumn leaves
Blown by the fitful rainy wind.
Thereon his final goal to find,
He lighted off his war-horse good
And let him wander as he would,
When he had eased him of his gear;
Then gathering heart against his fear.
Just at the silent end of day
Through the fair porch he took his way
And found at last a goodly hall
With glorious hangings on the wall,
Inwrought with trees of every clime,
And stories of the ancient time,
But all of sorcery they were.
For o'er the daïs Venus fair,
Fluttered about by many a dove,
Made hopeless men for hopeless love,
Both sick and sorry; there they stood
Wrought wonderfully in various mood,
But wasted all by that hid fire
Of measureless o'er-sweet desire,
And let the hurrying world go by
Forgetting all felicity.
But down the hall the tale was wrought
How Argo in old time was brought
To Colchis for the fleece of gold.
And on the other side was told
How mariners for long years came
To Circe, winning grief and shame.
Until at last by hardihead

And craft, Ulysses won her bed.
Long upon these the King did look
And of them all good heed he took;
To see if they would tell him aught
About the matter that he sought,
But all were of the times long past;
So going all about, at last
When grown nigh weary of his search
A falcon on a silver perch,
Anigh the daïs did he see,
And wondered, because certainly
At his first coming 'twas not there;
But 'neath the bird a scroll most fair,
With golden letters on the white
He saw, and in the dim twilight
By diligence could he read this:

"Ye who have not enow of bliss,
And in this hard world labour sore,
By manhood here may get you more,
And be fulfilled of everything,
Till ye be masters of the King.
And yet, since I who promise this
Am nowise God to give man bliss
Past ending, now in time beware,
And if you live in little care
Then turn aback and home again,
Lest unknown woe ye chance to gain
In wishing for a thing untried."

A little while did he abide,
When he had read this, deep in thought,
Wondering indeed if there were aught
He had not got, that a wise man
Would wish; yet in his mind it ran
That he might win a boundless realm,
Yea, come to wear upon his helm
The crown of the whole conquered earth;
That all who lived thereon, from birth
To death should call him King and Lord,
And great kings tremble at his word,
Until in turn he came to die.
Therewith a little did he sigh,
But thought, "Of Alexander yet
Men talk, nor would they e'er forget
My name, if this should come to be,
Whoever should come after me:
But while I lay wrapped round with gold
Should tales and histories manifold
Be written of me, false and true;
And as the time still onward drew

Almost a god would folk count me,
Saying, 'In our time none such be.'"
But therewith did he sigh again,
And said, "Ah, vain, and worse than vain!
For though the world forget me nought,
Yet by that time should I be brought
Where all the world I should forget,
And bitterly should I regret
That I, from godlike great renown,
To helpless death must fall adown:
How could I bear to leave it all?"
Then straight upon his mind did fall
Thoughts of old longings half forgot,
Matters for which his heart was hot
A while ago: whereof no more
He cared for some, and some right sore
Had vexed him, being fulfilled at last.
And when the thought of these had passed
Still something was there left behind,
That by no torturing of his mind
Could he in any language name,
Or into form of wishing frame.

At last he thought, "What matters it,
Before these seven days shall flit
Some great thing surely shall I find,
That gained will not leave grief behind,
Nor turn to deadly injury.
So now will I let these things be
And think of some unknown delight."

Now, therewithal, was come the night
And thus his watch was well begun;
And till the rising of the sun,
Waking, he paced about the hall,
And saw the hangings on the wall
Fade into nought, and then grow white
In patches by the pale moonlight,
And then again fade utterly
As still the moonbeams passed them by;
Then in a while, with hope of day,
Begin a little to grow grey,
Until familiar things they grew,
As up at last the great sun drew,
And lit them with his yellow light
At ending of another night
Then right glad was he of the day,
That passed with him in such-like way;
For neither man nor beast came near,
Nor any voices did he hear.
And when again it drew to night

Silent it passed, till first twilight
Of morning came, and then he heard
The feeble twittering of some bird,
That, in that utter silence drear,
Smote harsh and startling on his ear.
Therewith came on that lonely day
That passed him in no other way;
And thus six days and nights went by
And nothing strange had come anigh.
And on that day he well-nigh deemed
That all that story had been dreamed.
Daylight and dark, and night and day,
Passed ever in their wonted way;
The wind played in the trees outside,
The rooks from out the high trees cried;
And all seemed natural, frank, and fair,
With little signs of magic there.
Yet neither could he quite forget
That close with summer blossoms set,
And fruit hung on trees blossoming,
When all about was early spring.
Yea, if all this by man were made,
Strange was it that yet undecayed
The food lay on the tables still
Unchanged by man, that wine did fill
The golden cups, yet bright and red.
And all was so apparelléd
For guests that came not, yet was all
As though that servants filled the hall.
So waxed and waned his hopes, and still
He formed no wish for good or ill.
And while he thought of this and that
Upon his perch the falcon sat
Unfed, unhooded, his bright eyes
Beholders of the hard-earned prize,
Glancing around him restlessly,
As though he knew the time drew nigh
When this long watching should be done.

So little by little fell the sun,
From high noon unto sun-setting;
And in that lapse of time the King,
Though still he woke, yet none the less
Was dreaming in his sleeplessness
Of this and that which he had done
Before this watch he had begun;
Till, with a start, he looked at last
About him, and all dreams were past;
For now, though it was past twilight
Without, within all grew as bright
As when the noon-sun smote the wall,

Though no lamp shone within the hall.
Then rose the King upon his feet,
And well-nigh heard his own heart beat,
And grew all pale for hope and fear,
As sound of footsteps caught his ear
But soft, and as some fair lady,
Going as gently as might be,
Stopped now and then awhile, distraught
By pleasant wanderings of sweet thought.
Nigher the sound came, and more nigh,
Until the King unwittingly
Trembled, and felt his hair arise,
But on the door still kept his eyes.
That opened soon, and in the light
There stepped alone a lady bright,
And made straight toward him up the hall.
In golden garments was she clad
And round her waist a belt she had
Of emeralds fair, and from her feet,
That shod with gold the floor did meet,
She held the raiment daintily,
And on her golden head had she
A rose-wreath round a pearl-wrought crown,
Softly she walked with eyes cast down,
Nor looked she any other than
An earthly lady, though no man
Has seen so fair a thing as she.
So when her face the King could see
Still more he trembled, and he thought,
"Surely my wish is hither brought,
And this will be a goodly day
If for mine own I win this may."
And therewithal she drew anear
Until the trembling King could hear
Her very breathing, and she raised
Her head and on the King's face gazed
With serious eyes, and stopping there,
Swept from her shoulders her long hair,
And let her gown fall on her feet,
Then spoke in a clear voice and sweet:
"Well hast thou watched, so now, O King,
Be bold, and wish for some good thing;
And yet, I counsel thee, be wise.
Behold, spite of these lips and eyes,
Hundreds of years old now am I
And have seen joy and misery.
And thou, who yet hast lived in bliss.
I bid thee well consider this;
Better it were that men should live
As beasts, and take what earth can give,
The air, the warm sun and the grass

Until unto the earth they pass,
And gain perchance nought worse than rest
Than that not knowing what is best
For sons of men, they needs must thirst
For what shall make their lives accurst.
"Therefore I bid thee now beware,
Lest getting something seeming fair,
Thou com'st in vain to long for more
Or lest the thing thou wishest for
Make thee unhappy till thou diest,
Or lest with speedy death thou buyest
A little hour of happiness
Or lazy joy with sharp distress.
"Alas, why say I this to thee,
For now I see full certainly,
That thou wilt ask for such a thing,
It had been best for thee to fling
Thy body from a mountain-top,
Or in a white hot fire to drop,
Or ever thou hadst seen me here,
Nay then be speedy and speak clear."
Then the King cried out eagerly,
Grown fearless, "Ah, be kind to me!
Thou knowest what I long for then!
Thou know'st that I, a king of men,
Will ask for nothing else than thee!
Thou didst not say this could not be,
And I have had enough of bliss,
If I may end my life with this."
"Hearken," she said, "what men will say
When they are mad; before to-day
I knew that words such things could mean,
And wondered that it could have been.
"Think well, because this wished-for joy,
That surely will thy bliss destroy,
Will let thee live, until thy life
Is wrapped in such bewildering strife
That all thy days will seem but ill
Now wilt thou wish for this thing still?"
"Wilt thou then grant it?" cried the King;
"Surely thou art an earthly thing,
And all this is but mockery,
And thou canst tell no more than I
What ending to my life shall be."
"Nay, then," she said, "I grant it thee
Perforce; come nigh, for I am thine
Until the morning sun doth shine,
And only coming time can prove
What thing I am."
Dizzy with love,
And with surprise struck motionless

That this divine thing, with far less
Of striving than a village maid,
Had yielded, there he stood afraid,
Spite of hot words and passionate,
And strove to think upon his fate.

But as he stood there, presently
With smiling face she drew anigh,
And on his face he felt her breath.
"O love," she said, "dost thou fear death?
Not till next morning shalt thou die,
Or fall into thy misery."
Then on his hand her hand did fall,
And forth she led him down the hall,
Going full softly by his side.
"O love," she said, "now well betide
The day whereon thou cam'st to me.
I would this night a year might be,
Yea, life-long; such life as we have,
A thousand years from womb to grave."

And then that clinging hand seemed worth
Whatever joy was left on earth,
And every trouble he forgot,
And time and death remembered not:
Kinder she grew, she clung to him
With loving arms, her eyes did swim
With love and pity, as he strove
To show the wisdom of his love;
With trembling lips she praised his choice,
And said, "Ah, well may'st thou rejoice,
Well may'st thou think this one short night
Worth years of other men's delight.
If thy heart as mine own heart is,
Sunk in a boundless sea of bliss;
O love, rejoice with me! rejoice!"
But as she spoke, her honied voice
Trembled, and midst of sobs she said,
"O love, and art thou still afraid?
Return, then, to thine happiness,
Nor will I love thee any less;
But watch thee as a mother might
Her child at play."
With strange delight
He stammered out, "Nay, keep thy tears
for me, and for my ruined years
Weep love, that I may love thee more,
My little hour will soon be o'er."
"Ah, love," she said, "and thou art wise
As men are, with long miseries
Buying these idle words and vain,

My foolish love, with lasting pain;
And yet, thou wouldst have died at last
If in all wisdom thou hadst passed
Thy weary life: forgive me then,
In pitying the sad life of men."
Then in such bliss his soul did swim,
But tender music unto him
Her words were; death and misery
But empty names were grown to be,
As from that place his steps she drew,
And dark the hall behind them grew.

But end comes to all earthly bliss,
And by his choice full short was his;
And in the morning, grey and cold,
Beside the daïs did she hold
His trembling hand, and wistfully
He, doubting what his fate should be,
Gazed at her solemn eyes, that now,
Beneath her calm, untroubled brow,
Were fixed on his wild face and wan;
At last she said, "Oh, hapless man,
Depart! thy full wish hast thou had;
A little time thou hast been glad,
Thou shalt be sorry till thou die.
"And though, indeed, full fain am I
This might not be; nathless, as day
Night follows, colourless and grey,
So this shall follow thy delight,
Your joy hath ending with last night
Nay, peace, and hearken to thy fate.
"Strife without peace, early and late,
Lasting long after thou art dead,
And laid with earth upon thine head;
War without victory shalt thou have,
Defeat, nor honour shalt thou save;
Thy fair land shall be rent and torn,
Thy people be of all forlorn,
And all men curse thee for this thing."
She loosed his hand, but yet the King
Said, "Yea, and I may go with thee?
Why should we part? then let things be
E'en as they will!" "Poor man," she said,
"Thou ravest; our hot love is dead,
If ever it had any life:
Go, make thee ready for the strife
Wherein thy days shall soon be wrapped;
And of the things that here have happed
Make thou such joy as thou may'st do;
But I from this place needs must go,
Nor shalt thou ever see me more

Until thy troubled life is o'er:
Alas I to say 'farewell' to thee
Were nought but bitter mockery.
Fare as thou may'st, and with good heart
Play to the end thy wretched part."

Therewith she turned and went from him,
And with such pain his eyes did swim
He scarce could see her leave the place;
And then, with troubled and pale face,
He gat him thence: and soon he found
His good horse in the base-court bound;
So, loosing him, forth did he ride,
For the great gates were open wide,
And flat the heavy drawbridge lay.

So by the middle of the day,
That murky pass had he gone through,
And come to country that he knew;
And homeward turned his horse's head.
And passing village and homestead
Nigh to his palace came at last;
And still the further that he passed
From that strange castle of the fays,
More dreamlike seemed those seven days,
And dreamlike the delicious night;
And like a dream the shoulders white,
And clinging arms and yellow hair,
And dreamlike the sad morning there.
Until at last he 'gan to deem
That all might well have been a dream
Yet why was life a weariness?
What meant this sting of sharp distress?
This longing for a hopeless love,
No sighing from his heart could move?

Or else, 'She did not come and go
As fays might do, but soft and slow
Her lovely feet fell on the floor;
She set her fair hand to the door
As any dainty maid might do;
And though, indeed, there are but few
Beneath the sun as fair as she,
She seemed a fleshly thing to be.
Perchance a merry mock this is,
And I may some day have the bliss
To see her lovely face again,
As smiling she makes all things plain.
And then as I am still a king,
With me may she make tarrying
Full long, yea, till I come to die."

Therewith at last being come anigh
Unto his very palace gate,
He saw his knights and squires wait
His coming, therefore on the ground
He lighted, and they flocked around
Till he should tell them of his fare.
Then mocking said he, "Ye may dare,
The worst man of you all, to go
And watch as I was bold to do;
For nought I heard except the wind,
And nought I saw to call to mind."
So said he, but they noted well
That something more he had to tell
If it had pleased him; one old man,
Beholding his changed face and wan,
Muttered, "Would God it might be so!
Alas! I fear what fate may do;
Too much good fortune hast thou had
By anything to be more glad
Than thou hast been, I fear thee then
Lest thou becom'st a curse to men."
But to his place the doomed King passed,
And all remembrance strove to cast
From out his mind of that past day,
And spent his life in sport and play.

Great among other kings, I said
He was before he first was led
Unto that castle of the fays,
But soon he lost his happy days
And all his goodly life was done.
And first indeed his best-loved son,
The very apple of his eye,
Waged war against him bitterly;
And when this son was overcome
And taken, and folk led him home,
And him the King had gone to meet,
Meaning with gentle words and sweet
To win him to his love again,
By his own hand he found him slain.
I know not if the doomed King yet
Remembered the fay lady's threat,
But troubles upon troubles came:
His daughter next was brought to shame,
Who unto all eyes seemed to be
The image of all purity,
And fleeing from the royal place
The King no more beheld her face.
Then next a folk that came from far
Sent to the King great threats of war,
But he, full-fed of victory,

Deemed this a little thing to be,
And thought the troubles of his home
Thereby he well might overcome
Amid the hurry of the fight.
His foemen seemed of little might,
Although they thronged like summer bees
About the outlying villages,
And on the land great ruin brought.
Well, he this barbarous people sought
With such an army as seemed meet
To put the world beneath his feet;
The day of battle came, and he,
Flushed with the hope of victory,
Grew happy, as he had not been
Since he those glorious eyes had seen.
They met, his solid ranks of steel
There scarcely more the darts could feel
Of those new foemen, than if they
Had been a hundred miles away:
They met, a storied folk were his
To whom sharp war had long been bliss,
A thousand years of memories
Were flashing in their shielded eyes;
And grave philosophers they had
To bid them ever to be glad
To meet their death and get life done
Midst glorious deeds from sire to son.
And those they met were beasts, or worse,
To whom life seemed a jest, a curse;
Of fame and name they had not heard;
Honour to them was but a word,
A word spoke in another tongue;
No memories round their banners clung,
No walls they knew, no art of war,
By hunger were they driven afar
Unto the place whereon they stood,
Ravening for bestial joys and blood.

No wonder if these barbarous men
Were slain by hundreds to each ten
Of the King's brave well-armoured folk,
No wonder if their charges broke
To nothing, on the walls of steel,
And back the baffled hordes must reel.
So stood throughout a summer day
Scarce touched the King's most fair array,
Yet as it drew to even-tide
The foe still surged on every side,
As hopeless hunger-bitten men,
About his folk grown wearied then.
Therewith the King beheld that crowd

Howling and dusk, and cried aloud,
"What do ye, warriors? and how long
Shall weak folk hold in check the strong?
Nay, forward banners! end the day
And show these folk how brave men play."
The young knights shouted at his word,
But the old folk in terror heard
The shouting run adown the line,
And saw men flush as if with wine
"O Sire," they said, "the day is sure,
Nor will these folk the night endure
Beset with misery and fears."
Alas I they spoke to heedless ears;
For scarce one look on them he cast
But forward through the ranks he passed,
And cried out, "Who will follow me
To win a fruitful victory?"
And toward the foe in haste he spurred,
And at his back their shouts he heard,
Such shouts as he ne'er heard again.

They met, ere moonrise all the plain
Was filled by men in hurrying flight
The relics of that shameful fight;
The close array, the full-armed men,
The ancient fame availed not then,
The dark night only was a friend
To bring that slaughter to an end;
And surely there the King had died.
But driven by that back-rushing tide
Against his will he needs must flee;
And as he pondered bitterly
On all that wreck that he had wrought,
From time to time indeed he thought
Of the fay woman's dreadful threat.

"But everything was not lost yet;
Next day he said, great was the rout
And shameful beyond any doubt,
But since indeed at eventide
The flight began, not many died,
And gathering all the stragglers now
His troops still made a gallant show
Alas! it was a show indeed;
Himself desponding, did he lead
His beaten men against the foe,
Thinking at least to lie alow
Before the final rout should be
But scarce upon the enemy
Could these, whose shaken banners shook
The frightened world, now dare to look;

Nor yet could the doomed King die there
A death he once had held most fair;
Amid unwounded men he came
Back to his city, bent with shame,
Unkingly, midst his great distress,
Yea, weeping at the bitterness
Of women's curses that did greet
His passage down the troubled street
But sight of all the things they loved,
The memory of their manhood moved
Within the folk, and aged men
And boys must think of battle then.
And men that had not seen the foe
Must clamour to the war to go.
So a great army poured once more
From out the city, and before
The very gates they fought again,
But their late valour was in vain;
They died indeed, and that was good,
But nought they gained for all the blood
Poured out like water; for the foe,
Men might have stayed a while ago,
A match for very gods were grown,
So like the field in June-tide mown
The King's men fell, and but in vain
The remnant strove the town to gain;
Whose battlements were nought to stay
An untaught foe upon that day,
Though many a tale the annals told
Of sieges in the days of old,
When all the world then knew of war
From that fair place was driven afar.

As for the King, a charmed life
He seemed to bear; from out that strife
He came unhurt, and he could see,
As down the valley he did flee
With his most wretched company,
His palace flaming to the sky.
Then in the very midst of woe
His yearning thoughts would backward go
Unto the castle of the fay;
He muttered, "Shall I curse that day,
The last delight that I have had,
For certainly I then was glad?
And who knows if what men call bliss
Had been much better now than this
When I am hastening to the end."
That fearful rest, that dreaded friend,
That Death, he did not gain as yet;
A band of men he soon did get,

A ruined rout of bad and good,
With whom within the tangled wood,
The rugged mountain, he abode,
And thenceforth oftentimes they rode
Into the fair land once called his,
And yet but little came of this,
Except more woe for Heaven to see
Some little added misery
Unto that miserable realm:
The barbarous foe did overwhelm
The cities and the fertile plain,
And many a peaceful man was slain,
And many a maiden brought to shame.
And yielded towns were set aflame;
For all the land was masterless.
Long dwelt the King in great distress,
From wood to mountain ever tost,
Mourning for all that he had lost,
Until it chanced upon a day,
Asleep in early morn he lay,
And in a vision there did see
Clad all in black, that fay lady
Whereby all this had come to pass,
But dim as in a misty glass:
She said, "I come thy death to tell
Yet now to thee may say 'farewell,'
For in a short space wilt thou be
Within an endless dim country
Where thou may'st well win woe or bliss,"
Therewith she stooped his lips to kiss
And vanished straightway from his sight.
So waking there he sat upright
And looked around, but nought could see
And heard but song-birds' melody,
For that was the first break of day.

Then with a sigh adown he lay
And slept, nor ever woke again,
For in that hour was he slain
By stealthy traitors as he slept.
He of a few was much bewept,
But of most men was well forgot
While the town's ashes still were hot
The foeman on that day did burn.
As for the land, great Time did turn
The bloody fields to deep green grass,
And from the minds of men did pass
The memory of that time of woe,
And at this day all things are so
As first I said; a land it is
Where men may dwell in rest and bliss

If so they will. Who yet will not,
Because their hasty hearts are hot
With foolish hate, and longing vain
The sire and dam of grief and pain.

Neath the bright sky cool grew the weary earth,
And many a bud in that fair hour had birth
Upon the garden bushes; in the west
The sky got ready for the great sun's rest,
And all was fresh and lovely; none the less
Although those old men shared the happiness
Of the bright eve, 'twas mixed with memories
Of how they might in old times have been wise,
Not casting by for very wilfulness
What wealth might come their changing life to bless;
Lulling their hearts to sleep, amid the cold
Of bitter times, that so they might behold
Some joy at last, e'en if it lingered long.
That, wearing not their souls with grief and wrong,
They still might watch the changing world go by,
Content to live, content at last to die.
Alas! if they had reached content at last
It was perforce when all their strength was past;
And after loss of many days once bright,
With foolish hopes of unattained delight.

AUGUST

Across the gap made by our English hinds,
Amidst the Roman's handiwork, behold
Far off the long-roofed church; the shepherd binds
The withy round the hurdles of his fold;
Down in the foss the river fed of old,
That through long lapse of time has grown to be
The little grassy valley that you see.

Rest here awhile, not yet the eve is still,
The bees are wandering yet, and you may hear
The barley mowers on the trenchéd hill,
The sheep-bells, and the restless changing weir,
All little sounds made musical and clear
Beneath the sky that burning August gives.
While yet the thought of glorious Summer lives.

Ah, love! such happy days, such days as these,
Must we still waste them, craving for the best,
Like lovers o'er the painted images
Of those who once their yearning hearts have blessed?
Have we been happy on our day of rest?

Thine eyes say "yes," but if it came again,
Perchance its ending would not seem so vain.

Now came fulfilment of the year's desire,
The tall wheat, coloured by the August fire
Grew heavy-headed, dreading its decay,
And blacker grew the elm-trees day by day.
About the edges of the yellow corn,
And o'er the gardens grown somewhat outworn
The bees went hurrying to fill up their store;
The apple-boughs bent over more and more;
With peach and apricot the garden wall,
Was odorous, and the pears began to fall
From off the high tree with each freshening breeze.
So in a house bordered about with trees,
A little raised above the waving gold
The Wanderers heard this marvellous story told,
While 'twixt the gleaming flasks of ancient wine,
They watched the reapers' slow advancing line.

PYGMALION AND THE IMAGE

ARGUMENT

A man of Cyprus, a sculptor named Pygmalion, made an image of a woman, fairer than any that
had yet been seen, and in the end came to love his own handiwork as though it had been alive:
wherefore, praying to Venus for help, he obtained his end, for she made the image alive indeed,
and a woman, and Pygmalion wedded her.

At Amathus, that from the southern side
Of Cyprus, looks across the Syrian sea,
There did in ancient time a man abide
Known to the island-dwellers, for that he
Had wrought most godlike works in imagery,
And day by day still greater honour won,
Which man our old books call Pygmalion.

Yet in the praise of men small joy he had,
But walked abroad with downcast brooding face.
Nor yet by any damsel was made glad;
For, sooth to say, the women of that place
Must seem to all men an accursed race,
Who with the Turner of all Hearts once strove
And now their hearts must carry lust for love.

Upon a day it chanced that he had been
About the streets, and on the crowded quays,
Rich with unopened wealth of bales, had seen
The dark-eyed merchants of the southern seas

In chaffer with the base Propoetides,
And heavy-hearted gat him home again,
His once-loved life grown idle, poor, and vain.

And there upon his images he cast
His weary eyes, yet little noted them,
As still from name to name his swift thought passed.
For what to him was Juno's well-wrought hem,
Diana's shaft, or Pallas' olive-stem?
What help could Hermes' rod unto him give,
Until with shadowy things he came to live?

Yet note, that though, while looking on the sun,
The craftsman o'er his work some morn of spring
May chide his useless labour never done,
For all his murmurs, with no other thing
He soothes his heart, and dulls thought's poisonous sting,
And thus in thought's despite the world goes on;
And so it was with this Pygmalion.

Unto the chisel must he set his hand,
And slowly, still in troubled thought must pace,
About a work begun, that there doth stand,
And still returning to the self-same place,
Unto the image now must set his face,
And with a sigh his wonted toil begin,
Half-loathed, half-loved, a little rest to win.

The lessening marble that he worked upon,
A woman's form now imaged doubtfully,
And in such guise the work had he begun,
Because when he the untouched block did see
In wandering veins that form there seemed to be,
Whereon he cried out in a careless mood,
"O lady Venus, make this presage good!

"And then this block of stone shall be thy maid,
And, not without rich golden ornament,
Shall bide within thy quivering myrtle-shade."
So spoke he, but the goddess, well content,
Unto his hand such godlike mastery sent,
That like the first artificer he wrought,
Who made the gift that woe to all men brought.

And yet, but such as he was wont to do,
At first indeed that work divine he deemed,
And as the white chips from the chisel flew
Of other matters languidly he dreamed,
For easy to his hand that labour seemed,
And he was stirred with many a troubling thought,
And many a doubt perplexed him as he wrought.

And yet, again, at last there came a day
When smoother and more shapely grew the stone
And he, grown eager, put all thought away
But that which touched his craftsmanship alone,
And he would gaze at what his hands had done,
Until his heart with boundless joy would swell
That all was wrought so wonderfully well.

Yet long it was ere he was satisfied,
And with the pride that by his mastery
This thing was done, whose equal far and wide
In no town of the world a man could see,
Came burning longing that the work should be
E'en better still, and to his heart there came
A strange and strong desire he could not name.

The night seemed long, and long the twilight seemed,
A vain thing seemed his flowery garden fair;
Though through the night still of his work he dreamed,
And though his smooth-stemmed trees so nigh it were,
That thence he could behold the marble hair;
Nought was enough, until with steel in hand
He came before the wondrous stone to stand.

No song could charm him, and no histories
Of men's misdoings could avail him now,
Nay, scarcely seaward had he turned his eyes,
If men had said, "The fierce Tyrrhenians row
Up through the bay, rise up and strike a blow
For life and goods;" for nought to him seemed dear
But to his well-loved work to be anear.

Then vexed he grew, and knowing not his heart,
Unto himself he said, "Ah, what is this,
That I who oft was happy to depart,
And wander where the boughs each other kiss
'Neath the west wind, now have no other bliss
But in vain smoothing of this marble maid,
Whose chips this month a drachma had outweighed?

"Lo I will get me to the woods and try
If I my woodcraft have forgotten quite,
And then, returning, lay this folly by,
And eat my fill, and sleep my sleep anight,
And 'gin to carve a Hercules aright
Upon the morrow, and perchance indeed
The Theban will be good to me at need."

With that he took his quiver and his bow,
And through the gates of Amathus he went,

And toward the mountain slopes began to go,
Within the woods to work out his intent.
Fair was the day, the honied beanfield's scent
The west wind bore unto him, o'er the way
The glittering noisy poplar leaves did play.

All things were moving; as his hurried feet
Passed by, within the flowery swathe he heard
The sweeping of the scythe, the swallow fleet
Rose over him, the sitting partridge stirred
On the field's edge; the brown bee by him whirred,
Or murmured in the clover flowers below.
But he with bowed-down head failed not to go.

At last he stopped, and, looking round, he said,
"Like one whose thirtieth year is well gone by,
The day is getting ready to be dead;
No rest, and on the border of the sky
Already the great banks of dark haze lie;
No rest, what do I midst this stir and noise?
What part have I in these unthinking joys?"

With that he turned, and toward the city-gate
Through the sweet fields went swifter than he came,
And cast his heart into the hands of fate;
Nor strove with it, when higher 'gan to flame
That strange and strong desire without a name;
Till panting, thinking of nought else, once more
His hand was on the latch of his own door.

One moment there he lingered, as he said,
"Alas! what should I do if she were gone?"
But even with that word his brow waxed red
To hear his own lips name a thing of stone,
As though the gods some marvel there had done,
And made his work alive; and therewithal
In turn great pallor on his face did fall.

But with a sigh he passed into the house,
Yet even then his chamber-door must hold,
And listen there, half blind and timorous,
Until his heart should wax a little bold;
Then entering, motionless and white and cold,
He saw the image stand amidst the floor
All whitened now by labour done before.

Blinded with tears, his chisel up he caught,
And, drawing near, and sighing, tenderly
Upon the marvel of the face he wrought,
E'en as he used to pass the long days by;
But his sighs changed to sobbing presently,

And on the floor the useless steel he flung,
And, weeping loud, about the image clung.

"Alas!" he cried, "why have I made thee then,
That thus thou mockest me? I know indeed
That many such as thou are loved of men,
Whose passionate eyes poor wretches still will lead
Into their net, and smile to see them bleed;
But these the god's made, and this hand made thee
Who wilt not speak one little word to me."

Then from the image did he draw aback
To gaze on it through tears: and you had said,
Regarding it, that little did it lack
To be a living and most lovely maid;
Naked it was, its unbound locks were laid
Over the lovely shoulders; with one hand
Reached out, as to a lover, did it stand,

The other held a fair rose over-blown;
No smile was on the parted lips, the eyes
Seemed as if even now great love had shown
Unto them, something of its sweet surprise,
Yet saddened them with half-seen mysteries,
And still midst passion maiden-like she seemed,
As though of love unchanged for aye she dreamed.

Reproachfully beholding all her grace,
Pygmalion stood, until he grew dry-eyed,
And then at last he turned away his face
As if from her cold eyes his grief to hide;
And thus a weary while did he abide,
With nothing in his heart but vain desire,
The ever-burning, unconsuming fire.

But when again he turned his visage round
His eyes were brighter and no more he wept,
As if some little solace he had found,
Although his folly none the more had slept,
Rather some new-born god-sent madness kept
His other madness from destroying him,
And made the hope of death wax faint and dim;

For, trembling and ashamed, from out the street
Strong men he called, and faint with jealousy
He caused them bear the ponderous, moveless feet
Unto the chamber where he used to lie,
So in a fair niche to his bed anigh,
Unwitting of his woe, they set it down,
Then went their ways beneath his troubled frown.

Then to his treasury he went, and sought
Fair gems for its adornment, but all there
Seemed to his eager eyes but poor and nought,
Not worthy e'en to touch her rippled hair.
So he, departing, through the streets 'gan fare,
And from the merchants at a mighty cost
Bought gems that kings for no good deed had lost.

These then he hung her senseless neck around,
Set on her fingers, and fair arms of stone,
Then cast himself before her on the ground,
Praying for grace for all that he had done
In leaving her untended and alone;
And still with every hour his madness grew
Though all his folly in his heart he knew.

At last asleep before her feet he lay,
Worn out with passion, yet this burning pain
Returned on him, when with the light of day
He woke and wept before her feet again;
Then of the fresh and new-born morning fain,
Into his garden passed, and therefrom bore
New spoil of flowers his love to lay before.

A little altar, with fine gold o'erlaid,
Was in his house, that he a while ago
At some great man's command had deftly made,
And this he now must take and set below
Her well-wrought feet, and there must red flame glow
About sweet wood, and he must send her thence
The odour of Arabian frankincense.

Then as the smoke went up, he prayed and said,
"Thou, image, hear'st me not, nor wilt thou speak,
But I perchance shall know when I am dead,
If this has been some goddess' sport, to seek
A wretch, and in his heart infirm and weak
To set her glorious image, so that he,
Loving the form of immortality,

"May make much laughter for the gods above:
Hear me, and if my love misliketh thee
Then take my life away, for I will love
Till death unfeared at last shall come to me,
And give me rest, if he of might may be
To slay the love of that which cannot die,
The heavenly beauty that can ne'er pass by."

No word indeed the moveless image said,
But with the sweet grave eyes his hands had wrought
Still gazed down on his bowed imploring head,

Yet his own words some solace to him brought,
Gilding the net wherein his soul was caught
With something like to hope, and all that day
Some tender words he ever found to say;

And still he felt as something heard him speak;
Sometimes he praised her beauty, and sometimes
Reproached her in a feeble voice and weak,
And at the last drew forth a book of rhymes,
Wherein were writ the tales of many climes,
And read aloud the sweetness hid therein
Of lovers' sorrows and their tangled sin.

And when the sun went down, the frankincense
Again upon the altar-flame he cast
That through the open window floating thence
O'er the fresh odours of the garden passed;
And so another day was gone at last,
And he no more his love-lorn watch could keep,
But now for utter weariness must sleep.

But in the night he dreamed that she was gone,
And knowing that he dreamed, tried hard to wake
And could not, but forsaken and alone
He seemed to weep as though his heart would break,
And when the night her sleepy veil did take
From off the world, waking, his tears he found
Still wet upon the pillow all around.

Then at the first, bewildered by those tears,
He fell a-wondering wherefore he had wept,
But suddenly remembering all his fears,
Panting with terror, from the bed he leapt,
But still its wonted place the image kept,
Nor moved for all the joyful ecstasy
Wherewith he blessed the day that showed it nigh.

Then came the morning offering and the day,
Midst flowers and words of love and kisses sweet
From morn, through noon, to evening passed away,
And scarce unhappy, crouching at her feet
He saw the sun descend the sea to meet;
And scarce unhappy through the darkness crept
Unto his bed, and midst soft dreaming slept.

But the next morn, e'en while the incense-smoke
At sun-rising curled round about her head,
Sweet sound of songs the wonted quiet broke
Down in the street, and he by something led,
He knew not what, must leave his prayer unsaid,
And through the freshness of the morn must see

The folk who went with that sweet minstrelsy;

Damsels and youths in wonderful attire,
And in their midst upon a car of gold
An image of the Mother of Desire,
Wrought by his hands in days that seemed grown old
Though those sweet limbs a garment did enfold,
Coloured like flame, enwrought with precious things,
Most fit to be the prize of striving kings.

Then he remembered that the manner was
That fair-clad priests the lovely Queen should take
Thrice in the year, and through the city pass,
And with sweet songs the dreaming folk awake;
And through the clouds a light there seemed to break
When he remembered all the tales well told
About her glorious kindly deeds of old.

So his unfinished prayer he finished not,
But, kneeling, once more kissed the marble feet,
And, while his heart with many thoughts waxed hot,
He clad himself with fresh attire and meet
For that bright service, and with blossoms sweet
Entwined with tender leaves he crowned his head,
And followed after as the goddess led.

But long and vain unto him seemed the way
Until they came unto her house again;
Long years, the while they went about to lay
The honey-hiding dwellers on the plain,
The sweet companions of the yellowing grain
Upon her golden altar; long and long
Before, at end of their delicious song,

They stripped her of her weed with reverend hands
And showed the ivory limbs his hand had wrought;
Yea, and too long e'en then ere those fair bands,
Dispersing here and there, the shadow sought
Of Indian spice-trees o'er the warm sea brought
And toward the splashing of the fountain turned,
Mocked the noon sun that o'er the cloisters burned.

But when the crowd of worshippers was gone
And through the golden dimness of the place
The goddess' very servants paced alone,
Or some lone damsel murmured of her case
Apart from prying eyes, he turned his face
Unto that image made with toil and care,
In days when unto him it seemed most fair.

Dusky and dim, though rich with gems and gold,

The house of Venus was; high in the dome
The burning sun-light you could now behold,
From nowhere else the light of day might come,
To shame the Shame-faced Mother's lovely home;
A long way off the shrine, the fresh sea-breeze,
Now just arising, brushed the myrtle-trees.

The torches of the flower-crowned, singing band
Erewhile, indeed, made more than daylight there,
Lighting the painted tales of many a land,
And carven heroes, with their unused glare;
But now a few soft, glimmering lamps there were
And on the altar a thin, flickering flame
Just showed the golden letters of her name.

Blue in the dome yet hung the incense-cloud,
And still its perfume lingered all around;
And, trodden by the light-foot, fervent crowd,
Thick lay the summer flowers upon the ground,
And now from far-off halls uprose the sound
Of Lydian music, and the dancer's cry,
As though some door were opened suddenly.

So there he stood, some help from her to gain,
Bewildered by that twilight midst of day;
Downcast with listening to the joyous strain
He had no part in, hopeless with delay
Of all the fair things he had meant to say;
Yet, as the incense on the flame he cast,
From stammering lips and pale these words there passed,

"O thou forgotten help, dost thou yet know
What thing it is I need, when even I,
Bent down before thee in this shame and woe,
Can frame no set of words to tell thee why
I needs must pray, O help me or I die!
Or slay me, and in slaying take from me
Even a dead man's feeble memory.

"Say not thine help I have been slow to seek;
Here have I been from the first hour of morn,
Who stand before thy presence faint and weak,
Of my one poor delight left all forlorn;
Trembling with many fears, the hope outworn
I had when first I left my love, my shame,
To call upon thine oft-sung glorious name."

He stopped to catch his breath, for as a sob
Did each word leave his mouth; but suddenly,
Like a live thing, the thin flame 'gan to throb
And gather force, and then shot up on high

A steady spike of light, that drew anigh
The sunbeam in the dome, then sank once more
Into a feeble flicker as before.

But at that sight the nameless hope he had
That kept him living midst unhappiness,
Stirred in his breast, and with changed face and glad
Unto the image forward must he press
With words of praise his first word to redress,
But then it was as though a thick black cloud
Altar, and fire, and ivory limbs did shroud.

He staggered back, amazed and full of awe,
But when, with anxious eyes, he gazed around,
About him still the worshippers he saw
Sunk in their wonted works, with no surprise
At what to him seemed awful mysteries;
Therewith he sighed and said, "This, too, I dream,
No better day upon my life shall beam."

And yet for long upon the place he gazed
Where other folk beheld the lovely Queen;
And while he looked the dusky veil seemed raised,
And every thing was as it erst had been;
And then he said, "Such marvels I have seen
As some sick man may see from off his bed:
Ah, I am sick, and would that I were dead!"

Therewith, not questioning his heart at all,
He turned away and left the holy place,
When now the wide sun reddened towards his fall,
And a fresh west wind held the clouds in chase;
But coming out, at first he hid his face
Dazed with the light, and in the porch he stood,
Nor wished to move, or change his dreary mood.

Yet in a while the freshness of the eve
Pierced to his weary heart, and with a sigh
He raised his head, and slowly 'gan to leave
The high carved pillars; and so presently
Had passed the grove of whispering myrtles by,
And, mid the many noises of the street,
Made himself brave the eyes of men to meet.

Thronged were the ways with folk in gay attire,
Nursing the end of that festivity;
Girls fit to move the moody man's desire
Brushed past him, and soft dainty minstrelsy
He heard amid the laughter, and might see,
Through open doors, the garden's green delight,
Where pensive lovers waited for the night;

Or resting dancers round the fountain drawn,
With faces flushed unto the breeze turned round,
Or wandering o'er the fragrant trodden lawn,
Took up their fallen garlands from the ground,
Or languidly their scattered tresses bound,
Or let their gathered raiment fall adown,
With eyes downcast beneath their lovers' frown.

What hope Pygmalion yet might have, when he
First left the pillars of the dreamy place,
Amid such sights had vanished utterly.
He turned his weary eyes from face to face,
Nor noted them, as at a lagging pace
He gat towards home, and still was murmuring,
"Ah life, sweet life! the only godlike thing!"

And as he went, though longing to be there
Whereas his sole desire awaited him,
Yet did he loath to see the image fair,
White and unchanged of face, unmoved of limb,
And to his heart came dreamy thoughts and dim
That unto some strange region he might come,
Nor ever reach again his loveless home.

Yet soon, indeed, before his door he stood,
And, as a man awaking from a dream,
Seemed waked from his old folly; nought seemed good
In all the things that he before had deemed
At least worth life, and on his heart there streamed
Cold light of day, he found himself alone,
Reft of desire, all love and madness gone.

And yet for that past folly must he weep,
As one might mourn the parted happiness
That, mixed with madness, made him smile in sleep;
And still some lingering sweetness seemed to bless
The hard life left of toil and loneliness,
Like a past song too sweet, too short, and yet
Emmeshed for ever in the memory's net.

Weeping he entered, murmuring, "O fair Queen,
I thank thee that my prayer was not for nought,
Truly a present helper hast thou been
To those who faithfully thy throne have sought!
Yet, since with pain deliverance I have bought,
Hast thou not yet some gift in store for me,
That I thine happy slave henceforth may be?"

Thus to his chamber at the last he came,
And, pushing through the still half-opened door,

He stood within; but there, for very shame
Of all the things that he had done before,
Still kept his eyes bent down upon the floor,
Thinking of all that he had done and said
Since he had wrought that luckless marble maid.

Yet soft his thoughts were, and the very place
Seemed perfumed with some nameless heavenly air
So gaining courage, did he raise his face
Unto the work his hands had made so fair,
And cried aloud to see the niche all bare
Of that sweet form, while through his heart again
There shot a pang of his old yearning pain.

Yet while he stood, and knew not what to do
With yearning, a strange thrill of hope there came,
A shaft of new desire now pierced him through,
And therewithal a soft voice called his name,
And when he turned, with eager eyes aflame,
He saw betwixt him and the setting sun
The lively image of his lovéd one.

He trembled at the sight, for though her eyes,
Her very lips, were such as he had made,
And though her tresses fell but in such guise
As he had wrought them, now was she arrayed
In that fair garment that the priests had laid
Upon the goddess on that very morn,
Dyed like the setting sun upon the corn.

Speechless he stood, but she now drew anear,
Simple and sweet as she was wont to be,
And all at once her silver voice rang clear,
Filling his soul with great felicity,
And thus she spoke, "Pygmalion, come to me,
O dear companion of my new-found life,
For I am called thy lover and thy wife.

"Listen, these words the Dread One bade me say
That was with me e'en now, Pygmalion,
My new-made soul I give to thee to-day,
Come, feel the sweet breath that thy prayer has won,
And lay thine hand this heaving breast upon!
Come love, and walk with me between the trees,
And feel the freshness of the evening breeze.

"Sweep mine hair round thy neck; behold my feet,
The oft-kissed feet thou thoughtst should never move,
Press down the daisies! draw me to thee, sweet,
And feel the warm heart of thy living love
Beat against thine, and bless the Seed of Jove

Whose loving tender heart hath wrought all this,
And wrapped us both in such a cloud of bliss.

"Ah, thou art wise to know what this may mean!
Sweet seem the words to me, and needs must I
Speak all the lesson of the lovely Queen:
But this I know, I would we were more nigh,
I have not heard thy voice but in the cry
Thou utteredst then, when thou believedst gone
The marvel of thine hands, the maid of stone."

She reached her hand to him, and with kind eyes
Gazed into his; but he the fingers caught
And drew her to him, and midst ecstasies
Passing all words, yea, well-nigh passing thought,
Felt that sweet breath that he so long had sought,
Felt the warm life within her heaving breast
As in his arms his living love he pressed.

But as his cheek touched hers he heard her say,
"Wilt thou not speak, O love? why dost thou weep?
Art thou then sorry for this long-wished day,
Or dost thou think perchance thou wilt not keep
This that thou holdest, but in dreamy sleep?
Nay, let us do the bidding of the Queen,
And hand in hand walk through thy garden green;

"Then shalt thou tell me, still beholding me,
Full many things whereof I wish to know,
And as we walk from whispering tree to tree
Still more familiar to thee shall I grow,
And such things shalt thou say unto me now
As when thou deemedst thou wast quite alone,
A madman, kneeling to a thing of stone."

But at that word a smile lit up his eyes
And therewithal he spake some loving word,
And she at first looked up in grave surprise
When his deep voice and musical she heard,
And clung to him as grown somewhat afeard;
Then cried aloud and said, "O mighty one!
What joy with thee to look upon the sun."

Then into that fair garden did they pass
And all the story of his love he told,
And as the twain went o'er the dewy grass,
Beneath the risen moon could he behold
The bright tears trickling down, then, waxen bold,
He stopped and said, "Ah, love, what meaneth this?
Seest thou how tears still follow earthly bliss?"

Then both her white arms round his neck she threw
And sobbing said, "O love, what hurteth me?
When first the sweetness of my life I knew,
Not this I felt, but when I first saw thee
A little pain and great felicity
Rose up within me, and thy talk e'en now
Made pain and pleasure ever greater grow?"

"O sweet," he said, "this thing is even love,
Whereof I told thee; that all wise men fear,
But yet escape not; nay, to gods above,
Unless the old tales lie, it draweth near.
But let my happy ears I pray thee hear
Thy story too, and how thy blessed birth
Has made a heaven of this once lonely earth."

"My sweet," she said, "as yet I am not wise,
Or stored with words, aright the tale to tell,
But listen: when I opened first mine eyes
I stood within the niche thou knowest well,
And from mine hand a heavy thing there fell
Carved like these flowers, nor could I see things clear,
And but a strange confusèd noise could hear.

"At last mine eyes could see a woman fair,
But awful as this round white moon o'erhead.
So that I trembled when I saw her there,
For with my life was born some touch of dread,
And therewithal I heard her voice that said,
'Come down, and learn to love and be alive,
For thee, a well-prized gift, to-day I give.'

"Then on the floor I stepped, rejoicing much,
Not knowing why, not knowing aught at all,
Till she reached out her hand my breast to touch,
And when her fingers thereupon did fall,
Thought came unto my life, and therewithal
I knew her for a goddess, and began
To murmur in some tongue unknown to man.

"And then indeed not in this guise was I,
No sandals had I, and no saffron gown,
But naked as thou knowest utterly,
E'en as my limbs beneath thine hand had grown,
And this fair perfumed robe then fell adown
Over the goddess' feet and swept the ground,
And round her loins a glittering belt was bound.

"But when the stammering of my tongue she heard
Upon my trembling lips her hand she laid,
And spoke again, 'Nay, say not any word,

All that thine heart would say I know unsaid,
Who even now thine heart and voice have made;
But listen rather, for thou knowest now
What these words mean, and still wilt wiser grow.

"'Thy body, lifeless till I gave it life,
A certain man, my servant, well hath wrought
I give thee to him as his love and wife,
With all thy dowry of desire and thought,
Since this his yearning heart hath ever sought;
Now from my temple is he on the way,
Deeming to find thee e'en as yesterday;

"'Bide thou his coming by the bed-head there,
And when thou seest him set his eyes upon
Thine empty niche, and hear'st him cry for care,
Then call him by his name, Pygmalion,
And certainly thy lover hast thou won;
But when he stands before thee silently,
Say all these words that I shall teach to thee.'

"With that she said what first I told thee, love
And then went on, 'Moreover thou shalt say
That I, the daughter of almighty Jove,
Have wrought for him this long-desired day;
In sign whereof, these things that pass away,
Wherein mine image men have well arrayed,
I give thee for thy wedding gear, O maid.'

"Therewith her raiment she put off from her.
And laid bare all her perfect loveliness,
And, smiling on me, came yet more anear,
And on my mortal lips her lips did press,
And said, 'Now herewith shalt thou love no less
Than Psyche loved my son in days of old;
Farewell, of thee shall many a tale be told.'

"And even with that last word was she gone,
How, I know not, and I my limbs arrayed
In her fair gift, and waited thee alone
Ah, love, indeed the word is true she said,
For now I love thee so, I grow afraid
Of what the gods upon our heads may send
I love thee so, I think upon the end."

What words he said? How can I tell again
What words they said beneath the glimmering light,
Some tongue they used unknown to loveless men
As each to each they told their great delight,
Until for stillness of the growing night
Their soft sweet murmuring words seemed growing loud

And dim the moon grew, hid by fleecy cloud.

Such was the ending of his ancient rhyme,
That seemed to fit that soft and golden time,
When men were happy, they could scarce tell why,
Although they felt the rich year slipping by.
The sun went down, the harvest-moon arose,
And 'twixt the slim trees of that fruitful close
They saw the corn still falling 'neath its light,
While through the soft air of the windless night
The voices of the reapers' mates rang clear
In measured song, as of the fruitful year
They told, and its delights, and now and then
The rougher voices of the toiling men
Joined in the song, as one by one released
From that hard toil, they sauntered towards the feast
That waited them upon the strip of grass
That through the golden-glimmering sea did pass.
But those old men, glad to have lived so long,
Sat listening through the twilight to the song,
And when the night grew and all things were still
Throughout the wide vale from green hill to hill
Unto a happy harvesting they drank
Till once more o'er the hills the white moon sank.

August had not gone by, though now was stored
In the sweet-smelling granaries all the hoard
Of golden corn; the land had made her gain,
And winter should howl round her doors in vain.
But o'er the same fields grey now and forlorn
The old men sat and heard the swineherd's horn,
Far off across the stubble, when the day
At end of harvest-tide was sad and grey;
And rain was in the wind's voice as it swept
Along the hedges where the lone quail crept,
Beneath the chattering of the restless pie.
The fruit-hung branches moved, and suddenly
The trembling apples smote the dewless grass,
And all the year to autumn-tide did pass.
E'en such a day it was as young men love
When swiftly through the veins the blood doth move,
And they, whose eyes can see not death at all,
To thoughts of stirring deeds and pleasure fall,
Because it seems to them to tell of life
After the dreamy days devoid of strife,
When every day with sunshine is begun,
And cloudless skies receive the setting sun.
On such a day the older folk were fain
Of something new somewhat to dull the pain
Of sad, importunate old memories
That to their weary hearts must needs arise.

Alas! what new things on that day could come
From hearts that now so long had been the home
Of such dull thoughts, nay, rather let them tell
Some tale that fits their ancient longings well.
Rolf was the speaker, who said, "Friends, behold
This is e'en such a tale as those once told
Unto my greedy ears by Nicholas,
Before our quest for nothing came to pass."

OGIER THE DANE

ARGUMENT

When Ogier was born, six fay ladies came to the cradle where he lay, and gave him various gifts, as to be brave and happy and the like; but the sixth gave him to be her love when he should have lived long in the world: so Ogier grew up and became the greatest of knights, and at last, after many years, fell into the hands of that fay, and with her, as the story tells, he lives now, though he returned once to the world, as is shown in the process of this tale.

Within some Danish city by the sea,
Whose name, changed now, is all unknown to me,
Great mourning was there one fair summer eve,
Because the angels, bidden to receive
The fair Queen's lovely soul in Paradise,
Had done their bidding, and in royal guise
Her helpless body, once the prize of love,
Unable now for fear or hope to move,
Lay underneath the golden canopy;
And bowed down by unkingly misery
The King sat by it, and not far away,
Within the chamber a fair man-child lay,
His mother's bane, the king that was to be,
Not witting yet of any royalty,
Harmless and loved, although so new to life.

Calm the June evening was, no sign of strife
The clear sky showed, no storm grew round the sun,
Unhappy that his day of bliss was done;
Dumb was the sea, and if the beech-wood stirred,
'Twas with the nestling of the grey-winged bird
Midst its thick leaves; and though the nightingale
Her ancient, hapless sorrow must bewail,
No more of woe there seemed within her song
Than such as doth to lovers' words belong,
Because their love is still unsatisfied.
But to the King, on that sweet eventide,
No earth there seemed, no heaven when earth was gone;
No help, no God! but lonely pain alone;
And he, midst unreal shadows, seemed to sit

Himself the very heart and soul of it.
But round the cradle of the new-born child
The nurses now the weary time beguiled
With stories of the just departed Queen;
And how, amid the heathen folk first seen,
She had been won to love and godliness;
And as they spoke, e'en midst his dull distress,
An eager whisper now and then did smite
Upon the King's ear, of some past delight,
Some once familiar name, and he would raise
His weary head, and on the speaker gaze
Like one about to speak, but soon again
Would drop his head and be alone with pain,
Nor think of these; who, silent in their turn,
Would sit and watch the waxen tapers burn
Amidst the dusk of the quick-gathering night,
Until beneath the high stars' glimmering light,
The fresh earth lay in colourless repose.
So passed the night, and now and then one rose
From out her place to do what might avail
To still the new-born infant's fretful wail;
Or through the softly-opened door there came
Some nurse new waked, who, whispering low the name
Of her whose turn was come, would take her place;
Then toward the King would turn about her face
And to her fellows whisper of the day,
And tell again of her just past away.

So waned the hours, the moon arose and grew,
From off the sea a little west-wind blew,
Rustling the garden-leaves like sudden rain;
And ere the moon began to fall again
The wind grew cold, a change was in the sky,
And in deep silence did the dawn draw nigh:
Then from her place a nurse arose to light
Fresh hallowed lights, for, dying with the night,
The tapers round about the dead Queen were;
But the King raised his head and 'gan to stare
Upon her, as her sweeping gown did glide
About the floor, that in the stillness cried
Beneath her careful feet; and now as she
Had lit the second candle carefully,
And on its silver spike another one
Was setting, through her body did there run
A sudden tremor, and the hand was stayed
That on the dainty painted wax was laid;
Her eyelids fell down and she seemed to sleep,
And o'er the staring King began to creep
Sweet slumber too; the bitter lines of woe
That drew his weary face did softer grow,
His eyelids dropped, his arms fell to his side;

And moveless in their places did abide
The nursing women, held by some strong spell,
E'en as they were, and utter silence fell
Upon the mournful, glimmering chamber fair.
But now light footsteps coming up the stair,
Smote on the deadly stillness, and the sound
Of silken dresses trailing o'er the ground;
And heavenly odours through the chamber passed,
Unlike the scents that rose and lily cast
Upon the freshness of the dying night;
Then nigher drew the sound of footsteps light
Until the door swung open noiselessly
A mass of sunlit flowers there seemed to be
Within the doorway, and but pale and wan
The flame showed now that serveth mortal man,
As one by one six seeming ladies passed
Into the room, and o'er its sorrow cast
That thoughtless sense of joy bewildering,
That kisses youthful hearts amidst of spring;
Crowned were they, in such glorious raiment clad,
As yet no merchant of the world has had
Within his coffers; yet those crowns seemed fair
Only because they kissed their odorous hair,
And all that flowery raiment was but blessed
By those fair bodies that its splendour pressed.
Now to the cradle from that glorious band,
A woman passed, and laid a tender hand
Upon the babe, and gently drew aside
The swathings soft that did his body hide;
And, seeing him so fair and great, she smiled,
And stooped, and kissed him, saying, "O noble child,
Have thou a gift from Gloriande this day;
For to the time when life shall pass away
From this dear heart, no fear of death or shame,
No weariness of good shall foul thy name."
So saying, to her sisters she returned;
And one came forth, upon whose brow there burned
A crown of rubies, and whose heaving breast
With happy rings a golden hauberk pressed;
She took the babe, and somewhat frowning said,
"This gift I give, that till thy limbs are laid
At rest for ever, to thine honoured life
There never shall be lacking war and strife,
That thou a long-enduring name mayst win,
And by thy deeds, good pardon for thy sin."
With that another, who, unseen, meanwhile
Had drawn anigh, said with a joyous smile,
"And this forgotten gift to thee I give,
That while amidst the turmoil thou dost live,
Still shalt thou win the game, and unto thee
Defeat and shame but idle words shall be."

Then back they turned, and therewithal, the fourth
Said, "Take this gift for what it may be worth
For that is mine to give; lo, thou shalt be
Gentle of speech, and in all courtesy
The first of men: a little gift this is,
After these promises of fame and bliss."
Then toward the babe the fifth fair woman went;
Grey-eyed she was, and simple, with eyes bent
Down on the floor, parted her red lips were,
And o'er her sweet face marvellously fair
Oft would the colour spread full suddenly;
Clad in a dainty gown and thin was she,
For some green summer of the fay-land dight,
Tripping she went, and laid her fingers light
Upon the child, and said, "O little one,
As long as thou shalt look upon the sun
Shall women long for thee; take heed to this
And give them what thou canst of love and bliss."
Then, blushing for her words, therefrom she past,
And by the cradle stood the sixth and last,
The fairest of them all; awhile she gazed
Down on the child, and then her hand she raised,
And made the one side of her bosom bare;
"Ogier," she said, "if this be foul or fair
Thou know'st not now, but when thine earthly life
Is drunk out to the dregs, and war and strife
Have yielded thee whatever joy they may,
Thine head upon this bosom shalt thou lay;
And then, despite of knowledge or of God,
Will we be glad upon the flowery sod
Within the happy country where I dwell:
Ogier, my love that is to be, farewell!"

She turned, and even as they came they passed
From out the place, and reached the gate at last
That oped before their feet, and speedily
They gained the edges of the murmuring sea,
And as they stood in silence, gazing there
Out to the west, they vanished into air,
I know not how, nor whereto they returned.

But mixed with twilight in the chamber burned
The flickering candles, and those dreary folk,
Unlike to sleepers, from their trance awoke,
But nought of what had happed meanwhile they knew
Through the half-opened casements now there blew
A sweet fresh air, that of the flowers and sea
Mingled together, smelt deliciously,
And from the unseen sun the spreading light
Began to make the fair June blossoms bright,
And midst their weary woe uprose the sun,

And thus has Ogier's noble life begun.

Hope is our life, when first our life grows clear;
Hope and delight, scarce crossed by lines of fear,
Yet the day comes when fain we would not hope,
But forasmuch as we with life must cope,
Struggling with this and that, who knoweth why?
Hope will not give us up to certainty,
But still must bide with us: and with this man,
Whose life amid such promises began
Great things she wrought; but now the time has come
When he no more on earth may have his home.
Great things he suffered, great delights he had,
Unto great kings he gave good deeds for bad;
He ruled o'er kingdoms where his name no more
Is had in memory, and on many a shore
He left his sweat and blood to win a name
Passing the bounds of earthly creatures' fame.
A love he won and lost, a well-loved son
Whose little day of promise soon was done:
A tender wife he had, that he must leave
Before his heart her love could well receive;
Those promised gifts, that on his careless head
In those first hours of his fair life were shed
He took unwitting, and unwitting spent,
Nor gave himself to grief and discontent
Because he saw the end a-drawing nigh.
Where is he now? in what land must he die,
To leave an empty name to us on earth?
A tale half true, to cast across our mirth
Some pensive thoughts of life that might have been;
Where is he now, that all this life has seen?

Behold, another eve upon the earth
Than that calm evening of the warrior's birth;
The sun is setting in the west, the sky
Is bright and clear and hard, and no clouds lie
About the golden circle of the sun;
But East, aloof from him, heavy and dun
Steel-grey they pack with edges red as blood,
And underneath them is the weltering flood
Of some huge sea, whose tumbling hills, as they
Turn restless sides about, are black or grey,
Or green, or glittering with the golden flame;
The wind has fallen now, but still the same
The mighty army moves, as if to drown
This lone, bare rock, whose shear scarped sides of brown
Cast off the weight of waves in clouds of spray.
Alas! what ships upon an evil day
Bent over to the wind in this ill sea?
What navy, whose rent bones lie wretchedly

Beneath these cliffs? a mighty one it was,
A fearful storm to bring such things to pass.

This is the loadstone rock; no armament
Of warring nations, in their madness bent
Their course this way; no merchant wittingly
Has steered his keel unto this luckless sea;
Upon no shipman's card its name is writ,
Though worn-out mariners will speak of it
Within the ingle on the winter's night,
When all within is warm and safe and bright,
And the wind howls without: but 'gainst their will
Are some folk driven here, and then all skill
Against this evil rock is vain and nought,
And unto death the shipmen soon are brought;
For then the keel, as by a giant's hand,
Is drawn unto that mockery of a land,
And presently unto its sides doth cleave;
When if they 'scape swift death, yet none may leave
The narrow limits of that barren isle,
And thus are slain by famine in a while
Mocked, as they say, by night with images
Of noble castles among groves of trees,
By day with sounds of merry minstrelsy.

The sun sinks now below this hopeless sea,
The clouds are gone, and all the sky is bright;
The moon is rising o'er the growing night,
And by its shine may ye behold the bones
Of generations of these luckless ones
Scattered about the rock; but nigh the sea
Sits one alive, who uncomplainingly
Awaits his death. White-haired is he and old,
Arrayed in royal raiment, bright with gold,
But tarnished with the waves and rough salt air;
Huge is he, of a noble face and fair,
As for an ancient man, though toil and eld
Furrow the cheeks that ladies once beheld
With melting hearts. Nay, listen, for he speaks!
"God, Thou hast made me strong! nigh seven weeks
Have passed since from the wreck we haled our store,
And five long days well told, have now passed o'er
Since my last fellow died, with my last bread
Between his teeth, and yet I am not dead.
Yea, but for this I had been strong enow
In some last bloody field my sword to show.
What matter? soon will all be past and done,
Where'er I died I must have died alone:
Yet, Caraheu, a good death had it been
Dying, thy face above me to have seen,
And heard my banner flapping in the wind,

Then, though my memory had not left thy mind,
Yet hope and fear would not have vexed thee more
When thou hadst known that everything was o'er;
But now thou waitest, still expecting me,
Whose sail shall never speck thy bright blue sea.
"And thou, Clarice, the merchants thou mayst call,
To tell thee tales within thy pictured hall,
But never shall they tell true tales of me:
Whatever sails the Kentish hills may see
Swept by the flood-tide toward thy well-walled town,
No more on my sails shall they look adown.
"Get thee another leader, Charlemaine,
For thou shalt look to see my shield in vain,
When in the fair fields of the Frankish land,
Thick as the corn they tread, the heathen stand.
"What matter? ye shall learn to live your lives;
Husbands and children, other friends and wives,
Shall wipe the tablets of your memory clean,
And all shall be as I had never been.

"And now, O God, am I alone with Thee;
A little thing indeed it seems to be
To give this life up, since it needs must go
Some time or other; now at last I know
How foolishly men play upon the earth,
When unto them a year of life seems worth
Honour and friends, and these vague hopes and sweet
That like real things my dying heart do greet,
Unreal while living on the earth I trod,
And but myself I knew no other god.
Behold, I thank Thee that Thou sweet'nest thus
This end, that I had thought most piteous,
If of another I had heard it told."

What man is this, who weak and worn and old
Gives up his life within that dreadful isle,
And on the fearful coming death can smile?
Alas! this man, so battered and outworn,
Is none but he, who, on that summer morn,
Received such promises of glorious life:
Ogier the Dane this is, to whom all strife
Was but as wine to stir awhile the blood,
To whom all life, however hard, was good:
This is the man, unmatched of heart and limb,
Ogier the Dane, whose sight has waxed not dim
For all the years that he on earth has dwelt;
Ogier the Dane, that never fear has felt,
Since he knew good from ill; Ogier the Dane,
The heathen's dread, the evil-doer's bane.

Bright had the moon grown as his words were done,

And no more was there memory of the sun
Within the west, and he grew drowsy now.
And somewhat smoother was his wrinkled brow
As thought died out beneath the hand of sleep,
And o'er his soul forgetfulness did creep,
Hiding the image of swift-coming death;
Until as peacefully he drew his breath
As on that day, past for a hundred years,
When, midst the nurse's quickly-falling tears,
He fell asleep to his first lullaby.
The night changed as he slept, white clouds and high
Began about the lonely moon to close;
And from the dark west a new wind arose,
And with the sound of heavy-falling waves
Mingled its pipe about the loadstone caves;
But when the twinkling stars were hid away,
And a faint light and broad, like dawn of day,
The moon upon that dreary country shed,
Ogier awoke, and lifting up his head
And smiling, muttered, "Nay, no more again;
Rather some pleasure new, some other pain,
Unthought of both, some other form of strife;"
For he had waked from dreams of his old life,
And through St. Omer's archer-guarded gate
Once more had seemed to pass, and saw the state
Of that triumphant king; and still, though all
Seemed changed, and folk by other names did call
Faces he knew of old, yet none the less
He seemed the same, and, midst that mightiness,
Felt his own power, and grew the more athirst
For coming glory, as of old, when first
He stood before the face of Charlemaine,
A helpless hostage with all life to gain.
But now, awake, his worn face once more sank
Between his hands, and, murmuring not, he drank
The draught of death that must that thirst allay.

But while he sat and waited for the day
A sudden light across the bare rock streamed,
Which at the first he noted not, but deemed
The moon her fleecy veil had broken through;
But ruddier indeed this new light grew
Than were the moon's grey beams, and, therewithal
Soft far-off music on his ears did fall;
Yet moved he not, but murmured, "This is death.
An easy thing like this to yield my breath,
Awake, yet dreaming, with no sounds of fear,
No dreadful sights to tell me it is near;
Yea, God, I thank Thee!" but with that last word
It seemed to him that he his own name heard
Whispered, as though the wind had borne it past;

With that he gat unto his feet at last,
But still awhile he stood, with sunken head,
And in a low and trembling voice he said,
"Lord, I am ready, whither shall I go?
I pray Thee unto me some token show."
And, as he said this, round about he turned,
And in the east beheld a light that burned
As bright as day; then, though his flesh might fear
The coming change that he believed so near,
Yet did his soul rejoice, for now he thought
Unto the very heaven to be brought:
And though he felt alive, deemed it might be
That he in sleep had died full easily.
Then toward that light did he begin to go,
And still those strains he heard, far off and low,
That grew no louder; still that bright light streamed
Over the rocks, yet nothing brighter seemed,
But like the light of some unseen bright flame
Shone round about, until at last he came
Unto the dreary islet's other shore,
And then the minstrelsy he heard no more,
And softer seemed the strange light unto him,
But yet or ever it had grown quite dim,
Beneath its waning light could he behold
A mighty palace set about with gold,
Above green meads and groves of summer trees
Far-off across the welter of the seas;
But, as he gazed, it faded from his sight,
And the grey hidden moon's diffused soft light,
Which soothly was but darkness to him now,
His sea-girt island prison did but show.
But o'er the sea he still gazed wistfully,
And said, "Alas! and when will this go by
And leave my soul in peace? must I still dream
Of life that once so dear a thing did seem,
That, when I wake, death may the bitterer be?
Here will I sit until he come to me,
And hide mine eyes and think upon my sin,
That so a little calm I yet may win
Before I stand within the awful place."
Then down he sat and covered up his face.
Yet therewithal his trouble could not hide,
Nor waiting thus for death could he abide,
For, though he knew it not, the yearning pain
Of hope of life had touched his soul again
If he could live awhile, if he could live!
The mighty being, who once was wont to give
The gift of life to many a trembling man;
Who did his own will since his life began;
Who feared not aught, but strong and great and free
Still cast aside the thought of what might be;

Must all this then be lost, and with no will,
Powerless and blind, must he some fate fulfil,
Nor know what he is doing any more?

Soon he arose and paced along the shore,
And gazed out seaward for the blessed light;
But nought he saw except the old sad sight,
The ceaseless tumbling of the billows grey,
The white upspringing of the spurts of spray
Amidst that mass of timbers, the rent bones
Of the sea-houses of the hapless ones
Once cast like him upon this deadly isle.
He stopped his pacing in a little while,
And clenched his mighty hands, and set his teeth,
And gazing at the ruin underneath,
He swung from off the bare cliff's jagged brow,
And on some slippery ledge he wavered now,
Without a hand-hold, and now stoutly clung
With hands alone, and o'er the welter hung,
Not caring aught if thus his life should end;
But safely amidst all this did he descend
The dreadful cliff, and since no beach was there,
But from the depths the rock rose stark and bare,
Nor crumbled aught beneath the hammering sea,
Upon the wrecks he stood unsteadily.

But now, amid the clamour of the waves,
And washing to-and-fro of beams and staves,
Dizzy with hunger, dreamy with distress,
And all those days of fear and loneliness,
The ocean's tumult seemed the battle's roar,
His heart grew hot, as when in days of yore
He heard the cymbals clash amid the crowd
Of dusky faces; now he shouted loud,
And from crushed beam to beam began to leap,
And yet his footing somehow did he keep
Amidst their tossing, and indeed the sea
Was somewhat sunk upon the island's lee.
So quickly on from wreck to wreck he passed,
And reached the outer line of wrecks at last,
And there a moment stood unsteadily,
Amid the drift of spray that hurried by,
And drew Courtain his sword from out its sheath,
And poised himself to meet the coming death,
Still looking out to sea; but as he gazed,
And once or twice his doubtful feet he raised
To take the final plunge, that heavenly strain
Over the washing waves he heard again,
And from the dimness something bright he saw
Across the waste of waters towards him draw;
And hidden now, now raised aloft, at last

Unto his very feet a boat was cast,
Gilded inside and out, and well arrayed
With cushions soft; far fitter to have weighed
From some sweet garden on the shallow Seine,
Or in a reach of green Thames to have lain,
Than struggle with that huge confuséd sea;
But Ogier gazed upon it doubtfully
One moment, and then, sheathing Courtain, said,
"What tales are these about the newly dead
The heathen told? what matter, let all pass;
This moment as one dead indeed I was,
And this must be what I have got to do,
I yet perchance may light on something new
Before I die; though yet perchance this keel
Unto the wondrous mass of charméd steel
Is drawn as others." With that word he leapt
Into the boat, and o'er the cushions crept
From stem to stern, but found no rudder there,
Nor any oars, nor were the cushions fair
Made wet by any dashing of the sea.
Now while he pondered how these things could be,
The boat began to move therefrom at last,
But over him a drowsiness was cast,
And as o'er tumbling hills the skiff did pass,
He clean forgot his death and where he was.

At last he woke up to a sunny day,
And, looking round, saw that his shallop lay
Moored at the edge of some fair tideless sea
Unto an overhanging thick-leaved tree,
Where in the green waves did the low bank dip
Its fresh and green grass-covered daisied lip;
But Ogier looking thence no more could see
That sad abode of death and misery,
Nor aught but wide and empty ocean, grey
With gathering haze, for now it neared midday;
Then from the golden cushions did he rise,
And wondering still if this were Paradise
He stepped ashore, but drew Courtain his sword
And muttered therewithal a holy word.
Fair was the place, as though amidst of May,
Nor did the brown birds fear the sunny day,
For with their quivering song the air was sweet;
Thick grew the field-flowers underneath his feet,
And on his head the blossoms down did rain,
Yet mid these fair things slowly and with pain
He 'gan to go, yea, even when his foot
First touched the flowery sod, to his heart's root
A coldness seemed to strike, and now each limb
Was growing stiff, his eyes waxed bleared and dim,
And all his stored-up memory 'gan to fail,

Nor yet would his once mighty heart avail
For lamentations o'er his changéd lot;
Yet urged by some desire, he knew not what,
Along a little path 'twixt hedges sweet,
Drawn sword in hand, he dragged his faltering feet,
For what then seemed to him a weary way,
Whereon his steps he needs must often stay
And lean upon the mighty well-worn sword
That in those hands, grown old, for king or lord
Had small respect in glorious days long past.

But still he crept along, and at the last
Came to a gilded wicket, and through this
Entered a garden fit for utmost bliss,
If that might last which needs must soon go by:
There 'gainst a tree he leaned, and with a sigh
He said, "O God, a sinner I have been,
And good it is that I these things have seen
Before I meet what Thou hast set apart
To cleanse the earthly folly from my heart;
But who within this garden now can dwell
Wherein guilt first upon the world befell?"
A little further yet he staggered on,
Till to a fountain-side at last he won,
O'er which two white-thorns their sweet blossoms shed.
There he sank down, and laid his weary head
Beside the mossy roots, and in a while
He slept, and dreamed himself within the isle;
That splashing fount the weary sea did seem,
And in his dream the fair place but a dream;
But when again to feebleness he woke
Upon his ears that heavenly music broke,
Not faint or far as in the isle it was,
But e'en as though the minstrels now did pass
Anigh his resting-place; then fallen in doubt,
E'en as he might, he rose and gazed about,
Leaning against the hawthorn stem with pain;
And yet his straining gaze was but in vain,
Death stole so fast upon him, and no more
Could he behold the blossoms as before,
No more the trees seemed rooted to the ground,
A heavy mist seemed gathering all around,
And in its heart some bright thing seemed to be,
And round his head there breathed deliciously
Sweet odours, and that music never ceased.
But as the weight of Death's strong hand increased
Again he sank adown, and Courtain's noise
Within the scabbard seemed a farewell voice
Sent from the world he loved so well of old,
And all his life was as a story told,
And as he thought thereof he 'gan to smile

E'en as a child asleep, but in a while
It was as though he slept, and sleeping dreamed,
For in his half-closed eyes a glory gleamed,
As though from some sweet face and golden hair,
And on his breast were laid soft hands and fair,
And a sweet voice was ringing in his ears,
Broken as if with flow of joyous tears;
"Ogier, sweet friend, hast thou not tarried long?
Alas! thine hundred years of strife and wrong!"
Then he found voice to say, "Alas! dear Lord,
Too long, too long; and yet one little word
Right many a year agone had brought me here."
Then to his face that face was drawn anear,
He felt his head raised up and gently laid
On some kind knee, again the sweet voice said,
"Nay, Ogier, nay, not yet, not yet, dear friend!
Who knoweth when our linkéd life shall end,
Since thou art come unto mine arms at last,
And all the turmoil of the world is past?
Why do I linger ere I see thy face
As I desired it in that mourning place
So many years ago, so many years,
Thou knewest not thy love and all her fears?"
"Alas!" he said, "what mockery then is this
That thou wilt speak to me of earthly bliss?
No longer can I think upon the earth,
Have I not done with all its grief and mirth?
Yes, I was Ogier once, but if my love
Should come once more my dying heart to move,
Then must she come from 'neath the milk-white walls
Whereon to-day the hawthorn blossom falls
Outside St. Omer's, art thou she? her name
Which I remembered once mid death and fame
Is clean forgotten now; but yesterday,
Meseems, our son, upon her bosom lay:
Baldwin the fair, what hast thou done with him
Since Charlot slew him? All, mine eyes wax dim;
Woman, forbear! wilt thou not let me die?
Did I forget thee in the days gone by?
Then let me die, that we may meet again!"

He tried to move from her, but all in vain,
For life had well-nigh left him, but withal
He felt a kiss upon his forehead fall,
And could not speak; he felt slim fingers fair
Move to his mighty sword-worn hand, and there
Set on some ring, and still he could not speak,
And once more sleep weighed down his eyelids weak.

But, ah! what land was this he woke unto?
What joy was this that filled his heart anew?

Had he then gained the very Paradise?
Trembling, he durst not at the first arise,
Although no more he felt the pain of eld,
Nor durst he raise his eyes that now beheld
Beside him the white flowers and blades of grass;
He durst not speak, lest he some monster was.
But while he lay and hoped, that gentle voice
Once more he heard; "Yea, thou mayst well rejoice
Thou livest still, my sweet, thou livest still,
Apart from every earthly fear and ill;
Wilt thou not love me, who have wrought thee this,
That I like thee may live in double bliss?"
Then Ogier rose up, nowise like to one
Whose span of earthly life is nigh outrun,
But as he might have risen in old days
To see the spears cleave the fresh morning haze;
But, looking round, he saw no change there was
In the fair place wherethrough he first did pass,
Though all, grown clear and joyous to his eyes,
Now looked no worse than very Paradise;
Behind him were the thorns, the fountain fair
Still sent its glittering stream forth into air,
And by its basin a fair woman stood,
And as their eyes met his new-healéd blood
Rushed to his face; with unused thoughts and sweet
And hurrying hopes, his heart began to beat.
The fairest of all creatures did she seem;
So fresh and delicate you well might deem
That scarce for eighteen summers had she blessed
The happy, longing world; yet, for the rest,
Within her glorious eyes such wisdom dwelt
A child before her had the wise man felt,
And with the pleasure of a thousand years
Her lips were fashioned to move joy or tears
Among the longing folk where she might dwell,
To give at last the kiss unspeakable.
In such wise was she clad as folk may be,
Who, for no shame of their humanity,
For no sad changes of the imperfect year,
Rather for added beauty, raiment wear;
For, as the heat-foretelling grey-blue haze
Veils the green flowery morn of late May-days,
Her raiment veiled her; where the bands did meet
That bound the sandals to her dainty feet,
Gems gleamed; a fresh rose-wreath embraced her head,
And on her breast there lay a ruby red.
So with a supplicating look she turned
To meet the flame that in his own eyes burned,
And held out both her white arms lovingly,
As though to greet him as he drew anigh.
Stammering he said, "Who art thou? how am I

So cured of all my evils suddenly,
That certainly I felt no mightier, when,
Amid the backward rush of beaten men,
About me drooped the axe-torn Oriflamme?
Alas! I fear that in some dream I am."
"Ogier," she said, "draw near, perchance it is
That such a name God gives unto our bliss;
I know not, but if thou art such an one
As I must deem, all days beneath the sun
That thou hadst had, shall be but dreams indeed
To those that I have given thee at thy need.
For many years ago beside the sea
When thou wert born, I plighted troth with thee:
Come near then, and make mirrors of mine eyes,
That thou mayst see what these my mysteries
Have wrought in thee; surely but thirty years,
Passed amidst joy, thy new born body bears,
Nor while thou art with me, and on this shore
Art still full-fed of love, shalt thou seem more.
Nay, love, come nigher, and let me take thine hand,
The hope and fear of many a warring land,
And I will show thee wherein lies the spell,
Whereby this happy change upon thee fell."

Like a shy youth before some royal love,
Close up to that fair woman did he move,
And their hands met; yet to his changéd voice
He dared not trust; nay, scarcely could rejoice
E'en when her balmy breath he 'gan to feel,
And felt strange sweetness o'er his spirit steal
As her light raiment, driven by the wind,
Swept round him, and, bewildered and half-blind
His lips the treasure of her lips did press,
And round him clung her perfect loveliness.
For one sweet moment thus they stood, and then
She drew herself from out his arms again,
And panting, lovelier for her love, did stand
Apart awhile, then took her lover's hand,
And, in a trembling voice, made haste to say,
"O Ogier, when thou camest here to-day,
I feared indeed, that in my play with fate,
I might have seen thee e'en one day too late,
Before this ring thy finger should embrace;
Behold it, love, and thy keen eyes may trace
Faint figures wrought upon the ruddy gold;
My father dying gave it me, nor told
The manner of its making, but I know
That it can make thee e'en as thou art now
Despite the laws of God, shrink not from me
Because I give an impious gift to thee
Has not God made me also, who do this?

But I, who longed to share with thee my bliss,
Am of the fays, and live their changeless life,
And, like the gods of old, I see the strife
That moves the world, unmoved if so I will;
For we the fruit, that teaches good and ill,
Have never touched like you of Adam's race;
And while thou dwellest with me in this place
Thus shalt thou be, ah, and thou deem'st, indeed,
That thou shalt gain thereby no happy meed
Reft of the world's joys? nor canst understand
How thou art come into a happy land?
Love, in thy world the priests of heaven still sing,
And tell thee of it many a joyous thing;
But think'st thou, bearing the world's joy and pain,
Thou couldst live there? nay, nay, but born again
Thou wouldst be happy with the angels' bliss;
And so with us no otherwise it is,
Nor hast thou cast thine old life quite away
Even as yet, though that shall be to-day.
"But for the love and country thou hast won,
Know thou, that thou art come to Avallon,
That is both thine and mine; and as for me,
Morgan le Fay men call me commonly
Within the world, but fairer names than this
I have for thee and me, 'twixt kiss and kiss."

Ah, what was this? and was it all in vain,
That she had brought him here this life to gain?
For, ere her speech was done, like one turned blind
He watched the kisses of the wandering wind
Within her raiment, or as some one sees
The very best of well-wrought images
When he is blind with grief, did he behold
The wandering tresses of her locks of gold
Upon her shoulders; and no more he pressed
The hand that in his own hand lay at rest:
His eyes, grown dull with changing memories,
Could make no answer to her glorious eyes:
Cold waxed his heart, and weary and distraught,
With many a cast-by, hateful, dreary thought,
Unfinished in the old days; and withal
He needs must think of what might chance to fall
In this life new-begun; and good and bad
Tormented him, because as yet he had
A worldly heart within his frame made new,
And to the deeds that he was wont to do
Did his desires still turn. But she a while
Stood gazing at him with a doubtful smile,
And let his hand fall down; and suddenly
Sounded sweet music from some close nearby,
And then she spoke again: "Come, love, with me,

That thou thy new life and delights mayst see."
And gently with that word she led him thence,
And though upon him now there fell a sense
Of dreamy and unreal bewilderment,
As hand in hand through that green place they went,
Yet therewithal a strain of tender love
A little yet his restless heart did move.

So through the whispering trees they came at last
To where a wondrous house a shadow cast
Across the flowers, and o'er the daisied grass
Before it, crowds of lovely folk did pass,
Playing about in carelessness and mirth,
Unshadowed by the doubtful deeds of earth;
And from the midst a band of fair girls came,
With flowers and music, greeting him by name,
And praising him; but ever like a dream
He could not break, did all to Ogier seem.
And he his old world did the more desire,
For in his heart still burned unquenched the fire,
That through the world of old so bright did burn:
Yet was he fain that kindness to return,
And from the depth of his full heart he sighed.
Then toward the house the lovely Queen did guide
His listless steps, and seemed to take no thought
Of knitted brow or wandering eyes distraught,
But still with kind love lighting up her face
She led him through the door of that fair place,
While round about them did the damsels press;
And he was moved by all that loveliness
As one might be, who, lying half asleep
In the May morning, notes the light wind sweep
Over the tulip-beds: no more to him
Were gleaming eyes, red lips, and bodies slim,
Amidst that dream, although the first surprise
Of hurried love wherewith the Queen's sweet eyes
Had smitten him, still in his heart did stir.

And so at last he came, led on by her
Into a hall wherein a fair throne was,
And hand in hand thereto the twain did pass;
And there she bade him sit, and when alone
He took his place upon the double throne,
She cast herself before him on her knees,
Embracing his, and greatly did increase
The shame and love that vexed his troubled heart:
But now a line of girls the crowd did part,
Lovelier than all, and Ogier could behold
One in their midst who bore a crown of gold
Within her slender hands and delicate;
She, drawing nigh, beside the throne did wait

Until the Queen arose and took the crown,
Who then to Ogier's lips did stoop adown
And kissed him, and said, "Ogier, what were worth
Thy miserable days of strife on earth,
That on their ashes still thine eyes are turned?"
Then, as she spoke these words, his changed heart burned
With sudden memories, and thereto had he
Made answer, but she raised up suddenly
The crown she held and set it on his head,
"Ogier," she cried, "those troublous days are dead;
Thou wert dead with them also, but for me;
Turn unto her who wrought these things for thee!"
Then, as he felt her touch, a mighty wave
Of love swept o'er his soul, as though the grave
Did really hold his body; from his seat
He rose to cast himself before her feet;
But she clung round him, and in close embrace
The twain were locked amidst that thronging place.

Thenceforth new life indeed has Ogier won,
And in the happy land of Avallon
Quick glide the years o'er his unchanging head;
There saw he many men the world thought dead,
Living like him in sweet forgetfulness
Of all the troubles that did once oppress
Their vainly-struggling lives, ah, how can I
Tell of their joy as though I had been nigh?
Suffice it that no fear of death they knew,
That there no talk there was of false or true,
Of right or wrong, for traitors came not there;
That everything was bright and soft and fair,
And yet they wearied not for any change,
Nor unto them did constancy seem strange.
Love knew they, but its pain they never had,
But with each other's joy were they made glad;
Nor were their lives wasted by hidden fire,
Nor knew they of the unfulfilled desire
That turns to ashes all the joys of earth,
Nor knew they yearning love amidst the dearth
Of kind and loving hearts to spend it on,
Nor dreamed of discontent when all was won;
Nor need they struggle after wealth and fame;
Still was the calm flow of their lives the same,
And yet, I say, they wearied not of it
So did the promised days by Ogier flit.

Think that a hundred years have now passed by,
Since ye beheld Ogier lie down to die
Beside the fountain; think that now ye are
In France, made dangerous with wasting war;
In Paris, where about each guarded gate,

Gathered in knots, the anxious people wait,
And press around each new-come man to learn
If Harfleur now the pagan wasters burn,
Or if the Rouen folk can keep their chain,
Or Pont de l'Arche unburnt still guards the Seine?
Or if 'tis true that Andelys succour wants?
That Vernon's folk are fleeing east to Mantes?
When will they come? or rather is it true
That a great band the Constable o'erthrew
Upon the marshes of the lower Seine,
And that their long-ships, turning back again,
Caught by the high-raised waters of the bore
Were driven here and there and cast ashore?
Such questions did they ask, and, as fresh men
Came hurrying in, they asked them o'er again,
And from scared folk, or fools, or ignorant,
Still got new lies, or tidings very scant.

But now amidst these men at last came one,
A little ere the setting of the sun,
With two stout men behind him, armed right well,
Who ever as they rode on, sooth to tell,
With doubtful eyes upon their master stared,
Or looked about like troubled men and scared.
And he they served was noteworthy indeed;
Of ancient fashion were his arms and weed,
Rich past the wont of men in those sad times;
His face was bronzed, as though by burning climes,
But lovely as the image of a god
Carved in the days before on earth Christ trod;
But solemn were his eyes, and grey as glass,
And like to ruddy gold his fine hair was:
A mighty man he was, and taller far
Than those who on that day must bear the war
The pagans waged: he by the warders stayed
Scarce looked on them, but straight their words obeyed
And showed his pass; then, asked about his name
And from what city of the world he came,
Said, that men called him now the Ancient Knight,
That he was come midst the king's men to fight
From St. Omer's; and as he spoke, he gazed
Down on the thronging street as one amazed,
And answered no more to the questioning
Of frightened folk of this or that sad thing;
But, ere he passed on, turned about at last
And on the wondering guard a strange look cast,
And said, "St. Mary! do such men as ye
Fight with the wasters from across the sea?
Then, certes, are ye lost, however good
Your hearts may be; not such were those who stood
Beside the Hammer-bearer years agone."

So said he, and as his fair armour shone
With beauty of a time long passed away,
So with the music of another day
His deep voice thrilled the awe-struck, listening folk.

Yet from the crowd a mocking voice outbroke,
That cried, "Be merry, masters, fear ye nought,
Surely good succour to our side is brought;
For here is Charlemaine come off his tomb
To save his faithful city from its doom."
"Yea," said another, "this is certain news,
Surely ye know how all the carvers use
To carve the dead man's image at the best,
That guards the place where he may lie at rest;
Wherefore this living image looks indeed,
Spite of his ancient tongue and marvellous weed,
To have but thirty summers."
At the name
Of Charlemaine, he turned to whence there came
The mocking voice, and somewhat knit his brow,
And seemed as he would speak, but scarce knew how;
So with a half-sigh soon sank back again
Into his dream, and shook his well-wrought rein,
And silently went on upon his way.

And this was Ogier: on what evil day
Has he then stumbled, that he needs must come,
Midst war and ravage, to the ancient home
Of his desires? did he grow weary then,
And wish to strive once more with foolish men
For worthless things? or is fair Avallon
Sunk in the sea, and all that glory gone?
Nay, thus it happed. One day she came to him
And said, "Ogier, thy name is waxing dim
Upon the world that thou rememberest not;
The heathen men are thick on many a spot
Thine eyes have seen, and which I love therefore;
And God will give His wonted help no more.
Wilt thou, then, help? canst thou have any mind
To give thy banner once more to the wind?
Since greater glory thou shalt win for this
Than erst thou gatheredst ere thou cam'st to bliss:
For men are dwindled both in heart and frame,
Nor holds the fair land any such a name
As thine, when thou wert living midst thy peers;
The world is worser for these hundred years."
From his calm eyes there gleamed a little fire,
And in his voice was something of desire,
To see the land where he was used to be,
As now he answered: "Nay, choose thou for me,
Thou art the wisest; it is more than well

Within this peaceful place with thee to dwell:
Nor ill perchance in that old land to die,
If, dying, I keep not the memory
Of this fair life of ours." "Nay, nay," said she,
"As to thy dying, that shall never be,
Whiles that thou keep'st my ring, and now, behold,
I take from thee thy charmed crown of gold,
And thou wilt be the Ogier that thou wast
Ere on the loadstone rock thy ship was cast:
Yet thou shalt have thy youthful body still,
And I will guard thy life from every ill."

So was it done, and Ogier, armed right well,
Sleeping, was borne away by some strong spell,
And set upon the Flemish coast; and thence
Turned to St. Omer's, with a doubtful sense
Of being in some wild dream, the while he knew
That great delight forgotten was his due,
That all which there might hap was of small worth.
So on he went, and sometimes unto mirth
Did his attire move the country-folk,
But oftener when strange speeches from him broke
Concerning men and things for long years dead,
He filled the listeners with great awe and dread;
For in such wild times as these people were
Are men soon moved to wonder and to fear.

Now through the streets of Paris did he ride,
And at a certain hostel did abide
Throughout that night, and ere he went next day
He saw a book that on a table lay,
And opening it 'gan read in lazy mood:
But long before it in that place he stood,
Noting nought else; for it did chronicle
The deeds of men whom once he knew right well,
When they were living in the flesh with him:
Yea, his own deeds he saw, grown strange and dim
Already, and true stories mixed with lies,
Until, with many thronging memories
Of those old days, his heart was so oppressed,
He 'gan to wish that he might lie at rest,
Forgetting all things: for indeed by this
Little remembrance had he of the bliss
That wrapped his soul in peaceful Avallon.

But his changed life he needs must carry on;
For ye shall know the Queen was gathering men
To send unto the good King, who as then
In Rouen lay, beset by many a band
Of those who carried terror through the land,
And still by messengers for help he prayed:

Therefore a mighty muster was being made,
Of weak and strong, and brave and timorous,
Before the Queen anigh her royal house.
So thither on this morn did Ogier turn,
Some certain news about the war to learn;
And when he came at last into the square,
And saw the ancient palace great and fair
Rise up before him as in other days,
And in the merry morn the bright sun's rays
Glittering on gathered helms and moving spears,
He 'gan to feel as in the long-past years,
And his heart stirred within him. Now the Queen
Came from within, right royally beseen,
And took her seat beneath a canopy,
With lords and captains of the war anigh;
And as she came a mighty shout arose,
And round about began the knights to close,
Their oath of fealty to swear anew,
And learn what service they had got to do.
But so it was, that some their shouts must stay
To gaze at Ogier as he took his way
Through the thronged place; and quickly too he gat
Unto the place whereas the Lady sat,
For men gave place unto him, fearing him:
For not alone was he most huge of limb,
And dangerous, but something in his face,
As his calm eyes looked o'er the crowded place,
Struck men with awe; and in the ancient days,
When men might hope alive on gods to gaze,
They would have thought, "The gods yet love our town
And from the heavens have sent a great one down."
Withal unto the throne he came so near,
That he the Queen's sweet measured voice could hear;
And swiftly now within him wrought the change
That first he felt amid those faces strange;
And his heart burned to taste the hurrying life
With such desires, such changing sweetness rife.
And yet, indeed, how should he live alone,
Who in the old past days such friends had known?
Then he began to think of Caraheu,
Of Bellicent the fair, and once more knew
The bitter pain of rent and ended love.
But while with hope and vain regret he strove,
He found none 'twixt him and the Queen's high seat,
And, stepping forth, he knelt before her feet
And took her hand to swear, as was the way
Of doing fealty in that ancient day,
And raised his eyes to hers; as fair was she
As any woman of the world might be
Full-limbed and tall, dark-haired, from her deep eyes,
The snare of fools, the ruin of the wise,

Love looked unchecked; and now her dainty hand,
The well-knit holder of the golden wand,
Trembled in his, she cast her eyes adown,
And her sweet brow was knitted to a frown,
As he, the taker of such oaths of yore,
Now unto her all due obedience swore,
Yet gave himself no name; and now the Queen,
Awed by his voice as other folk had been,
Yet felt a trembling hope within her rise
Too sweet to think of, and with love's surprise
Her cheek grew pale; she said, "Thy style and name
Thou tellest not, nor what land of thy fame
Is glad; for, certes, some land must be glad,
That in its bounds her house thy mother had."
"Lady," he said, "from what far land I come
I well might tell thee, but another home
Have I long dwelt in, and its name have I
Forgotten now, forgotten utterly
Who were my fellows, and what deeds they did;
Therefore, indeed, shall my first name be hid
And my first country; call me on this day
The Ancient Knight, and let me go my way."
He rose withal, for she her fingers fair
Had drawn aback, and on him 'gan to stare
As one afeard; for something terrible
Was in his speech, and that she knew right well,
Who 'gan to love him, and to fear that she,
Shut out by some strange deadly mystery,
Should never gain from him an equal love;
Yet, as from her high seat he 'gan to move,
She said, "O Ancient Knight, come presently,
When we have done this muster, unto me,
And thou shalt have thy charge and due command
For freeing from our foes this wretched land!"
Then Ogier made his reverence and went,
And somewhat could perceive of her intent;
For in his heart life grew, and love with life
Grew, and therewith, 'twixt love and fame, was strife.
But, as he slowly gat him from the square,
Gazing at all the people gathered there,
A squire of the Queen's behind him came,
And breathless, called him by his new-coined name,
And bade him turn because the Queen now bade,
Since by the muster long she might be stayed,
That to the palace he should bring him straight,
Midst sport and play her coming back to wait;
Then Ogier turned, nought loath, and with him went,
And to a postern-gate his steps he bent,
That Ogier knew right well in days of old;
Worn was it now, and the bright hues and gold
Upon the shields above, with lapse of days,

Were faded much: but now did Ogier gaze
Upon the garden where he walked of yore,
Holding the hands that he should see no more;
For all was changed except the palace fair,
That Charlemaine's own eyes had seen built there
Ere Ogier knew him; there the squire did lead
The Ancient Knight, who still took little heed
Of all the things that by the way he said,
For all his thoughts were on the days long dead.
There in the painted hall he sat again,
And 'neath the pictured eyes of Charlemaine
He ate and drank, and felt it like a dream;
And midst his growing longings yet might deem
That he from sleep should wake up presently
In some fair city on the Syrian sea,
Or on the brown rocks of the loadstone isle.
But fain to be alone, within a while
He gat him to the garden, and there passed
By wondering squires and damsels, till at last,
Far from the merry folk who needs must play,
If on the world were coming its last day,
He sat him down, and through his mind there ran
Faint thoughts of that day, when, outworn and wan,
He lay down by the fountain-side to die.
But when he strove to gain clear memory
Of what had happed since on the isle he lay
Waiting for death, a hopeless castaway,
Thought, failing him, would rather bring again
His life among the peers of Charlemaine,
And vex his soul with hapless memories;
Until at last, worn out by thought of these,
And hopeless striving to find what was true,
And pondering on the deeds he had to do
Ere he returned, whereto he could not tell,
Sweet sleep upon his wearied spirit fell.
And on the afternoon of that fair day,
Forgetting all, beneath the trees he lay.

Meanwhile the Queen, affairs of state being done,
Went through the gardens with one dame alone
Seeking for Ogier, whom at last she found
Laid sleeping on the daisy-sprinkled ground.
Dreaming, I know not what, of other days.
Then on him for a while the Queen did gaze,
Drawing sweet poison from the lovely sight,
Then to her fellow turned, "The Ancient Knight
What means he by this word of his?" she said;
"He were well mated with some lovely maid
Just pondering on the late-heard name of love."
"Softly, my lady, he begins to move,"
Her fellow said, a woman old and grey;

"Look now, his arms are of another day;
None know him or his deeds; thy squire just said
He asked about the state of men long dead;
I fear what he may be; look, seest thou not
That ring that on one finger he has got,
Where figures strange upon the gold are wrought:
God grant that he from hell has not been brought
For our confusion, in this doleful war,
Who surely in enough of trouble are
Without such help;" then the Queen turned aside
Awhile, her drawn and troubled face to hide,
For lurking dread this speech within her stirred;
But yet she said, "Thou sayest a foolish word,
This man is come against our enemies
To fight for us." Then down upon her knees
Fell the old woman by the sleeping knight,
And from his hand she drew with fingers light
The wondrous ring, and scarce again could rise
Ere 'neath the trembling Queen's bewildered eyes
The change began; his golden hair turned white,
His smooth cheek wrinkled, and his breathing light
Was turned to troublous struggling for his breath,
And on his shrunk lips lay the hand of death;
And, scarce less pale than he, the trembling Queen
Stood thinking on the beauty she had seen
And longed for, but a little while ago,
Yet with her terror still her love did grow,
And she began to weep as though she saw
Her beauty e'en to such an ending draw.
And 'neath her tears waking he oped his eyes,
And strove to speak, but nought but gasping sighs
His lips could utter; then he tried to reach
His hand to them, as though he would beseech
The gift of what was his: but all the while
The crone gazed on them with an evil smile,
Then holding toward the Queen that wondrous ring,
She said, "Why weep'st thou? having this fair thing,
Thou, losing nought the beauty that thou hast,
May'st watch the vainly struggling world go past,
Thyself unchanged." The Queen put forth her hand
And took the ring, and there awhile did stand
And strove to think of it, but still in her
Such all-absorbing longings love did stir,
So young she was, of death she could not think,
Or what a cup eld gives to man to drink;
Yet on her finger had she set the ring
When now the life that hitherto did cling
To Ogier's heart seemed fading quite away,
And scarcely breathing with shut eyes he lay.
Then, kneeling down, she murmured piteously,
"Ah, wilt thou love me if I give it thee,

And thou grow'st young again? what should I do
If with the eyes thou thus shalt gain anew
Thou shouldst look scorn on me?" But with that word
The hedge behind her, by the west wind stirred,
Cast fear into her heart of some one nigh,
And therewith on his finger hastily
She set the ring, then rose and stood apart
A little way, and in her doubtful heart
With love and fear was mixed desire of life.
But standing so, a look with great scorn rife
The elder woman, turning, cast on her,
Pointing to Ogier, who began to stir;
She looked, and all she erst saw now did seem
To have been nothing but a hideous dream,
As fair and young he rose from off the ground
And cast a dazed and puzzled look around,
Like one just waked from sleep in some strange place;
But soon his grave eyes rested on her face,
And turned yet graver seeing her so pale,
And that her eyes were pregnant with some tale
Of love and fear; she 'neath his eyes the while
Forced her pale lips to semblance of a smile,
And said, "O Ancient Knight, thou sleepest then?
While through this poor land range the heathen men
Unmet of any but my King and Lord:
Nay, let us see the deeds of thine old sword."
"Queen," said he, "bid me then unto this work,
And certes I behind no wall would lurk,
Nor send for succour, while a scanty folk
Still followed after me to break the yoke:
I pray thee grace for sleeping, and were fain
That I might rather never sleep again
Then have such wretched dreams as I e'en now
Have waked from."
Lovelier she seemed to grow
Unto him as he spoke; fresh colour came
Into her face, as though for some sweet shame,
While she with tearful eyes beheld him so,
That somewhat even must his burnt cheek glow,
His heart beat faster. But again she said,
"Nay, will dreams burden such a mighty head?
Then may I too have pardon for a dream:
Last night in sleep I saw thee, who didst seem
To be the King of France; and thou and I
Were sitting at some great festivity
Within the many-peopled gold-hung place."
The blush of shame was gone as on his face
She gazed, and saw him read her meaning clear
And knew that no cold words she had to fear,
But rather that for softer speech he yearned.
Therefore, with love alone her smooth cheek burned;

Her parted lips were hungry for his kiss,
She trembled at the near approaching bliss;
Nathless, she checked her love a little while,
Because she felt the old dame's curious smile
Upon her, and she said, "O Ancient Knight,
If I then read my last night's dream aright,
Thou art come here our very help to be,
Perchance to give my husband back to me;
Come then, if thou this land art fain to save,
And show the wisdom thou must surely have
Unto my council; I will give thee then
What charge I may among my valiant men;
And certes thou wilt do so well herein,
That, ere long, something greater shalt thou win:
Come, then, deliverer of my throne and land,
And let me touch for once thy mighty hand
With these weak fingers."
                            As she spoke, she met
His eager hand, and all things did forget
But for one moment, for too wise were they
To cast the coming years of joy away;
Then with her other hand her gown she raised
And led him thence, and o'er her shoulder gazed
At her old follower with a doubtful smile,
As though to say, "Be wise, I know thy guile!"
But slowly she behind the lovers walked,
Muttering, "So be it! thou shalt not be balked
Of thy desire; be merry! I am wise,
Nor will I rob thee of thy Paradise
For any other than myself; and thou
May'st even happen to have had enow
Of this new love, before I get the ring,
And I may work for thee no evil thing."

Now ye shall know that the old chronicle,
Wherein I read all this, doth duly tell
Of all the gallant deeds that Ogier did,
There may ye read them; nor let me be chid
If I therefore say little of these things,
Because the thought of Avallon still clings
Unto my heart, and scarcely can I bear
To think of that long, dragging, useless year,
Through which, with dulled and glimmering memory,
Ogier was grown content to live and die
Like other men; but this I have to say,
That in the council chamber on that day
The Old Knight showed his wisdom well enow,
While fainter still with love the Queen did grow
Hearing his words, beholding his grey eyes
Flashing with fire of warlike memories;
Yea, at the last he seemed so wise indeed

That she could give him now the charge, to lead
One wing of the great army that set out
From Paris' gates, midst many a wavering shout,
Midst trembling prayers, and unchecked wails and tears,
And slender hopes and unresisted fears.

Now ere he went, upon his bed he lay,
Newly awakened at the dawn of day,
Gathering perplexéd thoughts of many a thing,
When, midst the carol that the birds did sing
Unto the coming of the hopeful sun,
He heard a sudden lovesome song begun
'Twixt two young voices in the garden green,
That seemed indeed the farewell of the Queen.

SONG

HÆC.
In the white-flowered hawthorn brake,
Love, be merry for my sake;
Twine the blossoms in my hair,
Kiss me where I am most fair
Kiss me, love! for who knoweth
What thing cometh after death?

ILLE.
Nay, the garlanded gold hair
Hides thee where thou art most fair;
Hides the rose-tinged hills of snow
Ah, sweet love, I have thee now!
Kiss me, love! for who knoweth
What thing cometh after death?

HÆC
Shall we weep for a dead day,
Or set Sorrow in our way?
Hidden by my golden hair,
Wilt thou weep that sweet days wear?
Kiss me, love! for who knoweth
What thing cometh after death?

ILLE.
Weep, O Love, the days that flit,
Now, while I can feel thy breath,
Then may I remember it
Sad and old, and near my death.
Kiss me, love! for who knoweth
What thing cometh after death?

Soothed by the pleasure that the music brought
And sweet desire, and vague and dreamy thought

Of happiness it seemed to promise him,
He lay and listened till his eyes grew dim,
And o'er him 'gan forgetfulness to creep
Till in the growing light he lay asleep,
Nor woke until the clanging trumpet-blast
Had summoned him all thought away to cast:
Yet one more joy of love indeed he had
Ere with the battle's noise he was made glad;
For, as on that May morning forth they rode
And passed before the Queen's most fair abode,
There at a window was she waiting them
In fair attire with gold in every hem,
And as the Ancient Knight beneath her passed
A wreath of flowering white-thorn down she cast,
And looked farewell to him, and forth he set
Thinking of all the pleasure he should get
From love and war, forgetting Avallon
And all that lovely life so lightly won;
Yea, now indeed the earthly life o'erpast
Ere on the loadstone rock his ship was cast
Was waxing dim, nor yet at all he learned
To 'scape the fire that erst his heart had burned.
And he forgat his deeds, forgat his fame,
Forgat the letters of his ancient name
As one waked fully shall forget a dream,
That once to him a wondrous tale did seem.

Now I, though writing here no chronicle
E'en as I said, must nathless shortly tell
That, ere the army Rouen's gates could gain
By a broad arrow had the King been slain,
And helpless now the wretched country lay
Beneath the yoke, until the glorious day
When Ogier fell at last upon the foe,
And scattered them as helplessly as though
They had been beaten men without a name:
So when to Paris town once more he came
Few folk the memory of the King did keep
Within their hearts, and if the folk did weep
At his returning, 'twas for joy indeed
That such a man had risen at their need
To work for them so great deliverance,
And loud they called on him for King of France.

But if the Queen's heart were the more a-flame
For all that she had heard of his great fame,
I know not; rather with some hidden dread
Of coming fate, she heard her lord was dead,
And her false dream seemed coming true at last,
For the clear sky of love seemed overcast
With clouds of God's great judgments, and the fear

Of hate and final parting drawing near.
So now when he before her throne did stand
Amidst the throng as saviour of the land,
And she her eyes to his kind eyes did raise,
And there before all her own love must praise;
Then did she fall a-weeping, and folk said,
"See, how she sorrows for the newly dead!
Amidst our joy she needs must think of him;
Let be, full surely shall her grief wax dim
And she shall wed again."
So passed the year,
While Ogier set himself the land to clear
Of broken remnants of the heathen men,
And at the last, when May-time came again,
Must he be crowned King of the twice-saved land,
And at the altar take the fair Queen's hand
And wed her for his own. And now by this
Had he forgotten clean the woe and bliss
Of his old life, and still was he made glad
As other men; and hopes and fears he had
As others, and bethought him not at all
Of what strange days upon him yet should fall
When he should live and these again be dead.

Now drew the time round when he should be wed,
And in his palace on his bed he lay
Upon the dawning of the very day:
'Twixt sleep and waking was he, and could hear
E'en at that hour, through the bright morn and clear,
The hammering of the folk who toiled to make
Some well-wrought stages for the pageant's sake,
Though hardly yet the sparrows had begun
To twitter o'er the coming of the sun,
Nor through the palace did a creature move.
There in the sweet entanglement of love
Midst languid thoughts of greater bliss he lay,
Remembering no more of that other day
Than the hot noon remembereth of the night,
Than summer thinketh of the winter white.
In that sweet hour he heard a voice that cried,
"Ogier, Ogier!" then, opening his eyes wide,
And rising on his elbow, gazed around,
And strange to him and empty was the sound
Of his own name; "Whom callest thou?" he said
"For I, the man who lie upon this bed,
Am Charles of France, and shall be King to-day,
But in a year that now is passed away
The Ancient Knight they called me: who is this,
Thou callest Ogier, then, what deeds are his?
And who art thou?" But at that word a sigh,
As of one grieved, came from some place anigh

His bed-side, and a soft voice spake again,
"This Ogier once was great amongst great men;
To Italy a helpless hostage led;
He saved the King when the false Lombard fled,
Bore forth the Oriflamme and gained the day;
Charlot he brought back, whom men led away,
And fought a day-long fight with Caraheu.
The ravager of Rome his right hand slew;
Nor did he fear the might of Charlemaine,
Who for a dreary year beset in vain
His lonely castle; yet at last caught then,
And shut in hold, needs must he come again
To give an unhoped great deliverance
Unto the burdened helpless land of France:
Denmark he gained thereafter, and he wore
The crown of England drawn from trouble sore;
At Tyre then he reigned, and Babylon
With mighty deeds he from the foemen won;
And when scarce aught could give him greater fame,
He left the world still thinking on his name.
"These things did Ogier, and these things didst thou,
Nor will I call thee by a new name now
Since I have spoken words of love to thee
Ogier, Ogier, dost thou remember me,
E'en if thou hast no thought of that past time
Before thou camest to our happy clime?"

As this was said, his mazed eyes saw indeed
A lovely woman clad in dainty weed
Beside his bed, and many a thought was stirred
Within his heart by that last plaintive word,
Though nought he said, but waited what should come
"Love," said she, "I am here to bring thee home;
Well hast thou done all that thou cam'st to do,
And if thou bidest here, for something new
Will folk begin to cry, and all thy fame
Shall then avail thee but for greater blame;
Thy love shall cease to love thee, and the earth
Thou lovest now shall be of little worth
While still thou keepest life, abhorring it
Behold, in men's lives that so quickly flit
Thus is it, how then shall it be with thee,
Who some faint image of eternity
Hast gained through me? alas, thou heedest not!
On all these changing things thine heart is hot
Take then this gift that I have brought from far,
And then may'st thou remember what we are;
The lover and the loved from long ago."
He trembled, and more memory seemed to grow
Within his heart as he beheld her stand,
Holding a glittering crown in her right hand:

"Ogier," she said, "arise and do on thee
The emblems of thy worldly sovereignty,
For we must pass o'er many a sea this morn."
He rose, and in the glittering tunic worn
By Charlemaine he clad himself, and took
The ivory hand, that Charlemaine once shook
Over the people's heads in days of old;
Then on his feet he set the shoes of gold.
And o'er his shoulders threw the mantle fair,
And set the gold crown on his golden hair:
Then on the royal chair he sat him down,
As though he deemed the elders of the town
Should come to audience; and in all he seemed
To do these things e'en as a man who dreamed.

And now adown the Seine the golden sun
Shone out, as toward him drew that lovely one
And took from off his head the royal crown,
And, smiling, on the pillow laid it down
And said, "Lie there, O crown of Charlemaine,
Worn by a mighty man, and worn in vain,
Because he died, and all the things he did
Were changed before his face by earth was hid;
A better crown I have for my love's head,
Whereby he yet shall live, when all are dead
His hand has helped." Then on his head she set
The wondrous crown, and said, "Forget, forget!
Forget these weary things, for thou hast much
Of happiness to think of."
At that touch
He rose, a happy light gleamed in his eyes;
And smitten by the rush of memories,
He stammered out, "O love! how came we here?
What do we in this land of Death and Fear?
Have I not been from thee a weary while?
Let us return, I dreamed about the isle;
I dreamed of other years of strife and pain,
Of new years full of struggles long and vain."
She took him by the hand and said, "Come, love,
I am not changed;" and therewith did they move
Unto the door, and through the sleeping place
Swiftly they went, and still was Ogier's face
Turned on her beauty, and no thought was his
Except the dear returning of his bliss.
But at the threshold of the palace-gate
That opened to them, she awhile did wait,
And turned her eyes unto the rippling Seine
And said, "O love, behold it once again!"
He turned, and gazed upon the city grey
Smit by the gold of that sweet morn of May;
He heard faint noises as of wakening folk

As on their heads his day of glory broke;
He heard the changing rush of the swift stream
Against the bridge-piers. All was grown a dream
His work was over, his reward was come,
Why should he loiter longer from his home?

A little while she watched him silently,
Then beckoned him to follow with a sigh,
And, raising up the raiment from her feet,
Across the threshold stepped into the street;
One moment on the twain the low sun shone,
And then the place was void, and they were gone
How I know not; but this I know indeed,
That in whatso great trouble or sore need
The land of France since that fair day has been,
No more the sword of Ogier has she seen.

Such was the tale he told of Avallon.
E'en such an one as in days past had won
His youthful heart to think upon the quest;
But to those old hearts nigh in reach of rest,
Not much to be desired now it seemed
Perchance the heart that of such things had dreamed
Had found no words in this death-laden tongue
We speak on earth, wherewith they might be sung;
Perchance the changing years that changed his heart
E'en in the words of that old tale had part,
Changing its sweet to bitter, to despair
The foolish hope that once had glittered there
Or think, that in some bay of that far home
They then had sat, and watched the green waves come
Up to their feet with many promises;
Or the light wind midst blossom-laden trees,
In the sweet Spring had weighted many a word
Of no worth now, and many a hope had stirred
Long dead for ever.

Howsoe'er that be
Among strange folk they now sat quietly,
As though that tale with them had nought to do,
As though its hopes and fears were something new
But though, indeed, the outworn, dwindled band
Had no tears left for that once longed-for land,
The very wind must moan for their decay,
And from the sky, grown dull, and low, and grey,
Cold tears must fall upon the lonely field,
That such fair golden hopes erewhile did yield;
And on the blackening woods, wherein the doves
Sat silent now, forgetful of their loves.
Yet, since a little life at least was left,
They were not yet of every joy bereft,

For long ago was past the agony,
Midst which they found that they indeed must die;
And now well-nigh as much their pain was past
As though death's veil already had been cast
Over their heads, so, midst some little mirth,
They watched the dark night hide the gloomy earth.

William Morris - A Short Biography

British poet, author, thinker and publisher William Morris was born in 1834 in Walthamstow, Essex. The eldest son of wealthy Londoners Emma Shelton Morris and William Morris, the younger Morris would become one of the most influential people in the cultural landscape of Victorian England.

Educated at home and at a nearby preparatory school, Morris's childhood was one of privilege, with books, leisurely excursions and ponies for personal use. The idyll ended (to an extent) with the sudden death of Morris Senior in 1847 when the younger Morris was just 14 years old. The next year, Morris began his formal studies at Marlborough College in Wiltshire. After three years of bullying and homesickness, Morris returned to his family home and was thereafter privately tutored.

In 1852, Morris entered Oxford University to study the Classics. While there he also became interested in medieval-era history and architecture. Morris would come to identify with medievalist ideals, as did a growing socio-political movement in England that rejected the values of the prevailing Victorian capitalist system. Morris would become even more politically active later in life, embracing the socialist values that he had recognized in medievalism as an undergraduate.

Morris made several important and life-long friends while at Exeter College at Oxford, most notably the artist and designer Edward Burne-Jones. Morris and Burne-Jones became part of a group of Oxford thinkers (most of them from the industrial city of Birmingham) who would be known historically as "The Birmingham Set." The group included divinity student William Fulford, poet and theologian Richard Watson Dixon, mathematician Charles Faulkner and scholar Cormell Price – internally they called themselves "The Brotherhood." The members of the group shared literary interests as well as values and were huge fans of Alfred Lord Tennyson, art critic John Ruskin, the Arthurian legends and William Shakespeare.

In 1856, Morris helped fund and start up the *Oxford and Cambridge Magazine*, the first of many cooperative projects in which he took an active role. Twelve issues were published. Also in 1856 – upon completion of his Bachelor of Arts degree - Morris was apprenticed briefly to the Oxford based Gothic revival architect George Edmund Street. Morris would use lessons learned from Street, and supervising architect Philip Webb, during the design process for his own Red House in Kent. Morris lived there with his new family – wife Jane Burdon, who he married in 1859, and daughters Jenny and Mary – until 1865.

In 1858 Morris published *The Defence of Guenvere*, an innovative volume of lyric and dramatic verse, which nonetheless was not well received critically. Morris would not publish again until 1867 when Bell and Dandy published the epic romantic poem *The Life and Death of Jason*. The printing was financed by Morris himself; happily, the book was well received and Morris received a fee for the second edition.

From 1861 Morris commuted from The Red House to London where he had opened a decorative arts firm with Burne-Jones, Webb, Faulkner and other friends: the Pre-Raphaelite painter Dante Gabriel Rossetti, Ford Madox Brown and Peter Paul Marshall. The company – known publicly as Morris, Marshall, Faulkner & Co. and privately as "The Firm" – specialized in locally produced fabrics, furniture, tapestries, wallpaper, architectural carving and stained glass windows. In 1875, Morris assumed total control of the company, now named Morris & Co. Though known in his lifetime chiefly for being a poet, Morris would also achieve posthumous acclaim as a chief architect of the "Arts and Crafts" British design movement.

In 1865, Morris sold The Red House and moved to Bloomsbury in London with his family. By 1870, he was a cultural fixture in that city and a celebrity of some stature.

From 1865 to 1870, Morris worked on another epic poem, *The Earthly Paradise*. Designed as homage to Chaucer, it consists of 24 stories, each with a different narrator from a different cultural background. Set in the late 14th century, it is about a group of Norsemen who flee the Black Death by sailing away from Europe, on the way discovering an island where the inhabitants continue to venerate an ancient Greek god. Published in four parts by F. S. Ellis, the epic gained a cult following and established Morris' reputation as a major poet.

Greatly influenced by his friendship with Icelandic theologian Eiríkr Magnússon and several visits to Iceland, Morris produced a series of English-language translations of the Icelandic Eddas and Sagas (old Norse poems and stories). Morris also taught himself calligraphy and created hand written copies of Nordic tales in translation, including *Frithiof the Bold* and *Halfden the Black*. It was the continuation of a life-long devotion to craft, a feature of many of his subsequent works, including the poetic drama *Love is Enough*, published in 1872 with woodcut illustrations by Burne-Jones.

Though leading a rich life in London, Morris did find the city unhealthy for his young family. He came across and fell in love with a 16th century manor house in Oxfordshire. The Morris family would share Kelmscott Manor with Morris' friend Rossetti (who, it is said, had developed a close relationship with Morris' wife Jane) until their friendship eventually disintegrated. Kelmscott also lent its name to another of Morris' achievements – the Kelmscott Press, which he co-founded, with Emery Walker, in 1891. The bespoke publishing house was dedicated to publishing limited edition, illuminated style fine art books, in keeping with Morris' devotion to the craft of making books as beautiful objects. The Press dovetailed with Morris' continuing design work with Morris & Co. Over the next seven years, it would publish 66 volumes, the first of which was Morris' own novel, *The Story of the Glittering Plain*, in 1891. The Kelmscott Press would go on to publish 23 of Morris' books, but also editions of works by Keats, Shelley, Ruskin, and Swinburne, as well as copies of various Medieval texts. Kelmscott's magnum opus would turn out to be the Kelmscott Chaucer, published in 1896; it took several years to complete and included 87 illustrations and decorative borders from Burne-Jones.

In 1883, Morris joined England's first socialist organization, the Democratic Federation, later renamed the Socialist Democratic Federation (SDF). This was the beginning of years of overt activism on behalf of workers and the poor. In 1884, Morris and a large group of SDF members seceded in order to form the brand new Socialist League (SL). For the rest of the decade, Morris worked tirelessly for the cause; he met several times each week with his comrades from the SL and delivered hundreds of lectures. He was arrested in 1885 for disorderly conduct at the trial of several Socialist protesters, wrote for and edited SL's newspaper, *The Commonweal* and wrote a long series of socialist literary works, including the song collection *Chants for Socialists* (1884); a narrative poem, *The Pilgrims of Hope* (1885); the historical meditation *A Dream of John Ball* (1887); and his most influential work, *News from Nowhere* (1890), a pastoral utopian communist vision of England in the twenty-first century.

Morris also continued as a poet and prose writer. In December 1888, the Chiswick Press published his *The House of the Wolfings*, a fantasy story set in Iron Age Europe, which provides a reconstructed portrait of the lives of Germanic-speaking Gothic tribes. The book contains both prose and poetic verse and was followed by a two-volume sequel, *The Roots of the Mountains*, in 1899.

Morris also embarked on a translation of the quintessential Anglo-Saxon tale, *Beowulf*. Because he could not fully understand Old English, his poetic translation was based largely on that already produced by A.J. Watts. *The Tale of Beowulf* was not well received.

In the last nine years of his life, Morris wrote a series of imaginative fictions usually referred to as the "prose romances." These novels – including *The Wood Beyond the World* and *The Well at the World's End* (1896) – have been credited as important milestones in the history of fantasy fiction, because, while other writers wrote of foreign lands, or of dream worlds, or the future (as Morris had already done in the utopian *News from Nowhere*), Morris's works were the first to be set in an entirely invented neo-medieval fantasy world.

By 1896, Morris was an invalid, not working much but being visited by friends and family at his home. The great man died of tuberculosis on October 4th, 1896. Morris' funeral was held on October 6th, his corpse carried from Kelmscott House, his home in Hammersmith, to Paddington rail station, where it was transported to Oxford, then to Kelmscott, where it was buried in the churchyard of St. George's Church.

Morris lives on with the legacy of the Arts and Crafts movement, in his many fine literary works, essays and translations and through his homes, which have been preserved by the UK's National Trust and the William Morris Society as monuments to the man and the epic period of cultural history in which he flourished.

William Morris - A Concise Bibliography

Collected Poetry, Fiction, and Essays
The Hollow Land (1856)
The Defence of Guenevere, and other Poems (1858)
The Life and Death of Jason (1867)
The Earthly Paradise (1868–1870)
Love is Enough, or The Freeing of Pharamond: A Morality (1872)
The Story of Sigurd the Volsung and the Fall of the Niblungs (1877)
Hopes and Fears For Art (1882)
The Pilgrims of Hope (1885)
A Dream of John Ball (1888)
A Tale of the House of the Wolfings, and All the Kindreds of the Mark. In Prose and in Verse (1889)
The Roots of the Mountains (1890)
Poems By the Way (1891)
News from Nowhere (or, An Epoch of Rest) (1890)
The Story of the Glittering Plain (1891)
The Wood Beyond the World (1894)
Child Christopher and Goldilind the Fair (1895)

The Well at the World's End (1896)
The Water of the Wondrous Isles (1897)
The Sundering Flood (1897)
A King's Lesson (1901)
The World of Romance (1906)
Chants for Socialists (1935)

Translations

Grettis Saga: The Story of Grettir the Strong with Eiríkr Magnússon (1869)
The Saga of Gunnlaug the Worm-tongue and Rafn the Skald with Eiríkr Magnússon (1869)
Völsung Saga: The Story of the Volsungs and Niblungs, with Certain Songs from the Elder Eddawith Eiríkr Magnússon (1870) (from the Volsunga saga)
Three Northern Love Stories & Other Tales with Eiríkr Magnússon (1875)
The Odyssey of Homer Done into English Verse (1887)
The Aeneids of Virgil Done into English (1876)
Of King Florus and the Fair Jehane (1893)
The Tale of Beowulf Done out of the Old English Tongue (1895)
Old French Romances Done into English (1896)

Published Lectures and Papers

Lectures on Art delivered in support of the Society for the Protection of Ancient Buildings (Morris lecture on The Lesser Arts). London, Macmillan, 1882
Architecture and History & Westminster Abbey". Papers read to SPAB in 1884 and 1893. Printed at The Chiswick Press. London, Longmans, 1900
Communism: a lecture London, Fabian Society, 1903

www.ingramcontent.com/pod-product-compliance
Lightning Source LLC
LaVergne TN
LVHW051055080426
835508LV00019B/1894